What "Friends oj Bill Are Saying

"If true, the allegations about the president's relationship with Monica Lewinsky show that he failed to meet the standards of character he set for himself, and shattered the promise he made to the public and the people around him. Right now, I don't know whether to be angry, sad or both. But if the Lewinsky charges are valid, I know this: I'm livid. It's a terrible waste of years of work by thousands of people with the support of millions more."

—*George Stephanopoulus, Former Clinton Advisor*

"If the allegations are true... how is it this intelligent, ambitious, politically savvy man can be so foolhardy and such a slave to his libido?"
—*Katie Couric, The Today Show*

"Why haven't the soccer moms decided to throw Clinton out of the (White) House? Why are the Democratic women pols who shot off their mouths about Clarence Thomas, holding their tongues about Bill? And, above all, why aren't feminists who put sexual harassment on the office bulletin board standing by their Monica?"
—*Ellen Goodman, Syndicated Columnist*

"I think, however, like I said, when it comes to role models—I mean Bill Clinton is a role model to our teenagers. Is he saying to them it's OK to mess around when you're married and commit adultery? I don't think that's an example to set for our youngsters." —*Gennifer Flowers*

"Now, frustrated and angered by his inability to issue a flat-out denial devoid of linguistic tricks, the crowd lives with the uneasy knowledge that they have a terribly flawed man in the White House whom they trust with the economy but not with their own daughters."
—*Mike Barnicle, Boston Globe*

"They [feminists] were not in full throat when James Carville suggested Paula Jones was trailer trash, when Bob Bennett compared Paula Jones to a dog, when Clintonites wrote up talking points to discredit Kathleen Willey, and when the Clinton attack team roughed up Ms. Lewinsky... Funny, I thought feminism was devised to root out all those "he's a stud, she's a slut" double standards."
—*Maureen Dowd, The New York Times*

"[M]ost varieties of philandering by middle-aged big shots imply a willingness to use women in a way that suggests an exploitative attitude toward people in general."

—*Michael Kinsley, A Proud Liberal*

"But I will give you this. I'll be the first to admit... that if these charges that have been levied against President Clinton turn out to be true... If the president did these things, he ought to be dealt with and dealt with severely."

—*Tavis Smiley, Author of* **Hard Left: Straight Talk about the Wrongs of the Right**

"In electing Clinton, voters entered an implicit bargain: "We promise to forgive your past; you promise to behave in the future. If you have a psychological problem with sex, please get help." Exploiting an intern would not only be wrong but would violate the covenant."

—*David Gergen, Former Clinton Aide*

"We'd probably give the president low marks in the morals department, but then we don't see him as our moral leader. He was elected to run the country. We'll worry about our morals ourselves, thank you very much."

—*Thomas BeVier, USA Today*

"There isn't another shoe to drop in the discussion of the President's sex life. There's a whole closet full of pumps, slingbacks, spikes, flats, wedgies, sandals, and boots."

—*Michael Kelly,* **The New Republic**

"Ms. Lewinsky must die so that the women of America can have better child care, longer maternity stays, toll-free domestic violence hot lines and bustling mutual funds. Mrs. Clinton knows she can count on the complicity of feminists and Democratic women in Congress. They accept the trade-off in letting a few women be debased so that they can get more day-care centers."

—*Maureen Down,* **The New York Times**

"It's mystifying to me that someone with so much to offer and so much to lose would risk everything in such a reckless way."

—*George Stephanopoulus, Former Clinton Advisor*

SCANDALGATE

Exposing America's
Moral
Deficit Disorder

———

KENNETH J. BROWN

Legacy Communications Group, Inc.
Franklin, Tennessee

*To my parents, Bob and Betty, who instilled in me
a belief that character matters.
Thank you for living a life worth imitating.*

*To my lovely daughters, Rachel and Julie, two young
women who have the kind of character that matters.
Thank you for living your lives in ways that make it
very easy for your parents to be proud of you.*

CONTENTS

Introduction

"**S**o, it really is 'the economy, stupid,'" blared the cover story of *USA Today* on February 2, 1998. In a couple of brief paragraphs two crack reporters delivered the goods. They served up a stinging indictment of the moral climate in postmodern America during Bill Clinton's watch:

> Twelve days into the seamiest and most sensational scandal to face a sitting president, Americans gave him an approval rating of 69% in a *USA Today/CNN/*Gallup Poll taken Friday through Sunday.
>
> Never mind that only 39% of the people say he's setting a good moral example for the country. President Clinton is on a roll: 78% approve of the way he's managing the government, 76% approve of his positions on major issues, 74% are confident in his

ability to carry out his duties, and 65% have a favorable view of him.[1]

Just over one-third of those polled thought the president of the United States offered "a good moral example" to the country. And to "the children." But more than three-quarters of those same folks told pollsters that they approved of the way that the president did his job. "He can run the country," they opined, "so we'll cut him some slack if he runs around on Hillary." Here was proof, in black and white, that Americans have accepted the masquerade of postmodern morality. Actually, the term "postmodern morality" is an oxymoron. There is no such animal. It is the amoral precept of our postmodern political culture that is at issue—that a person's private conduct doesn't shape his conduct in a public office.

One person who sniffed the aromas of this amoral soup condensed it into a form that most people could digest. Gertrude Himmelfarb explained it this way for readers of the *New York Times:*

> Although he has not been formally charged with wrongdoing, the President is on trial—in the court of public opinion .... At first the public was discreet, professing to defer judgment until all the evidence was in. But with each revelation, more and more people have come to believe that the President is indeed guilty of sexual impropriety of some kind with "that woman," as he has referred to Monica Lewinsky.

At the same time, many insist that this judgment is not only premature, but also irrelevant. Such alleged affairs, they say, are private and have no bearing on the President's conduct as President—whereupon they proceed to bestow on him the highest approval ratings of his career.[2]

Privately, people joke about the president's sexual peccadilloes. But publicly, many still try to laugh off the stark reality of the claims that the president is a sexual predator. What they admit in private conversation, they deny in public discourse. As a former editor of the *New Republic* (hardly a vehicle for right-wing propaganda), Michael Kelly defied that practice. He made it clear that he believes Mr. Clinton is an Oval Office Romeo:

> There isn't another shoe to drop in the discussion of the President's sex life. There's a whole closet full of pumps, slingbacks, spikes, flats, wedgies, sandals, and boots.[3]

If most people would be honest in public about their private doubts, they would have to agree with Mr. Kelly. There is not much question that the allegations about Monica Lewinsky and Kathleen Willey are true. As comedian Bill Maher concedes, there is "an O.J. level of evidence there for that."[4] Only one question remains in regard to these allegations. Not whether they are true or not. But will there ever be rock-solid, guilty-verdict-type proof that they are true?

There is not much reason to question whether the President did what has been alleged. But there is a great reason to question whether the American people are right to dismiss it as inconsequential. "So he did it!" the approval polls shrug. "Big deal! Tell me something I don't know." Whether the president ever faces a trial in a court of law—or in the Congress—over the Lewinsky and Willey affairs, one thing is incontrovertible. It is the American public that has been put on trial before a grand jury of its own peers.

Gertrude Himmelfarb saw this clearly:

> The defining moment in every historic trial—the Dreyfus case, most notably, or the O.J. Simpson case—comes when it is no longer the defendant who is on trial, but the public.[5]

At question is whether the American people have served, or are willing to serve, as the president's co-conspirator in his role as First Sex Addict. Are we willing to accept a sexual predator as the commander-in-chief of the same army that considered court-martial charges against its highest-ranking enlisted soldier for being a sexual predator? Is it not ironic that the trial of Sergeant-Major McKinney took place in a military courtroom while his commander-in-chief was on trial in the court of public opinion?

How should we respond to the amoral code of conduct

presented to us as a nation in this postmodern era? Can we say with a straight face that what a person does in private has zero effect on what that same person does in public? Do we really believe that? Chapter 1 of this book raises the question, "If character doesn't matter, what does?" Answering that question brings us face-to-face with a practical and seemingly intractable objection: "But John F. Kennedy did it!" Ah, there's the rub. Other presidents have cheated on their wives, and they got away with it. John F. Kennedy was probably the first First Sex Addict. If "we the people" tolerated this behavior in former presidents, how can we confront this president on the same issue? Chapter 2 will grapple with that objection.

Some people have given voice to another objection: "If Hillary doesn't care, why should we?" If the First Couple has a way of handling the president's predatory behavior, why shouldn't we learn to wink at it? Chapter 3 will address that question. But that raises a different question. Even if the First Feminist doesn't care if her husband uses women and then tosses them aside like old shoes, shouldn't other feminists care? Where are the voices of protests from other feminists? Why is there such a deafening silence from that quarter? They joined Anita Hill's bandwagon, but have abandoned Paula Jones and Kathleen Willey to the wolves (or the First Wolf). Chapter 4 will examine the question, "Where is N.O.W. now?"

Many people have admitted that they believe Mr. Clinton is guilty of having sex with a White House intern. But they have shrugged that off. Then, faced with the question of whether the president lied about this affair, they shrug that off, too. "Doesn't everybody lie about sex?" they carp, smiling like Cheshire cats. But are "those irksome non-denial denials" not part of a pattern of dissembling that has characterized this administration? Chapter 5 will deal with that question.

Some people have speculated that Bill Clinton has a deeper coating of Teflon than the original "Teflon president", Ronald Reagan. But is Mr. Clinton, as his former fellow sex-addict Dick Morris once said, "an Achilles without a heel"? In Chapter 6 that question raises the alarming prospect of what we have to look forward to if Bill Clinton gets away with his predatory behavior. It is kind of ironic, isn't it? When the Clinton Administration sponsored the "Don't ask, don't tell" policy for gays in the military, many people didn't realize that it would also prove to be a cover for the commander-in-chief in his own sexual behavior. Chapter 7 argues that "Don't ask, don't tell" doesn't cut it!

Have you noticed that once again the best defense was a ruthless offense? In order to sidetrack the public from focusing on Mr. Clinton's behavior, the Clinton attack machine shifted the focus to Ken Starr's investigation. "When all else fails... attack Ken Starr" has been a common practice for this White House. In Chapter 8 this practice will be investigated. Chapter 9 will analyze another fall-out of the president's sexcapades. Jay Leno, David Letterman, Bill Maher, and an endless parade of comedians have been able to make a living by poking fun at Bill Clinton's sex life. Is the presidency a joke, or just this president? Which is it?

Finally, in Chapter 10, you will find an overview of the scandalous sexual behavior of President Clinton. In a review of his sexcapades there will be an attempt to show that there was much more to the Lewinsky story than whether the President received sexual favors from a White House intern. As if that shouldn't have been enough. But there is something more diabolical at work here than even that. This scandal, combined with all of the other Clinton scandals, is part of a pattern of an abuse of power that dwarfs Watergate. Sexgate or Watergate II? Which gets your vote?

In a bold assessment of President John F. Kennedy entitled, *A Question of Character,* Thomas Reeves warned that this nation must learn its lesson. We can't allow ourselves to be charmed by slick images, like those of Camelot. If we do allow ourselves to be charmed by another candidate's charisma, Reeves wrote in 1991, the results could be horrifying. Did Mr. Reeves have a premonition about William Jefferson Clinton?

In our longing to find heroes in a greedy, anonymous, and insensitive age, we might once more be swayed by someone who is wonderfully attractive, has a glib tongue, a bottomless wallet, and a conscience that asks little and demands even less. And the target of our affections might be much worse than Jack Kennedy.[6]

Do you believe this?

"Clinton is not necessarily a good man.
His relationship with Monica may ultimately prove that.
But that fact does not mean he is incapable of imbuing
his politics and policies with good values."[7]
—*Nashville Scene*

If Character Doesn't Matter, What Does?

Even in a breaking news story this was breaking news. CNN, MSNBC, CNBC, ABC, NBC, and CBS all were repeatedly reporting that President Clinton had admitted to having an affair with Gennifer Flowers in his deposition for the Paula Jones lawsuit. Despite what many people had perceived as a denial of the affair on *60 Minutes* six years ago, the President now had admitted to it. Larry King wasted no time in getting Gennifer Flowers on his program as soon as possible.

In the heart of the interview with Ms. Flowers, Larry pointed out that President Kennedy's "popularity keeps going up" even after the latest exposé by Seymour Hersch, *The Dark Side of Camelot.* Implication? People don't care about the sexual escapades of the president. Having concluded that, Larry asked, "Do you think the public doesn't want to be lied to, but sex is a private matter?" Ms. Flowers objected:

> Well, I think in general, it can be a private matter unless it has to do with our role models. And I think that they have a huge responsibility to be moral. And certainly if indeed—well, he did participate in an adulterous relationship with me, and that's not against our laws, but it's against God's laws. And I don't think it's something that he should have been doing or would be doing now or anyone else...

Larry interrupted Gennifer in mid-sentence to temper her remarks with this observation: "Many high-powered politicians have done this in their life. Sex and Washington is a...." Flowers interrupted his thought in return, objecting:

> But that doesn't make it right. And I think if something ultimately huge happens about this, it will be an example set to say, this kind of stuff has got to stop. And we, the American people, are not going to accept it anymore, really.

Larry tried to wrestle her at that point for control of the interview. He seemed a little surprised to have the "scarlet woman" preach a sermon about adultery on his show. Once again he tried to temper the force of her moral argument with a restatement of the postmodern moral code. "Are you surprised that 60 percent polled feel that private matters should be private?" he asked Ms. Flowers. "And they may want the president to—but they just believe that what you do behind your door is your business."

Gennifer hedged a little, agreeing that "what consenting adults do behind closed doors is their business." But then she bounced back to her point that the president of the United States should be a role model.

> I think, however, like I said, when it comes to role models—I mean Bill Clinton is a role model to our teenagers. Is he saying to them it's OK to mess around when you're married and commit adultery? I don't think that's an example to se. for our youngsters.

At that point Larry King surrendered. Raising the white flag, he asked meekly, "So character counts?" Ms. Flowers didn't hesitate to answer. "Absolutely." "Even if the wife forgives?" Larry asked. To which Gennifer proclaimed, "Even if the wife forgives, character definitely counts."

Imagine that. A woman stained with the "scarlet letter" preaching to the country that adultery is wrong. Was that unseemly? Or was it noteworthy? Was it hypocritical on her part to say this kind of thing? Or did this remarkable "Live" conversation suggest that she has had a change of heart? It is against "God's laws," she insisted. Does she have the right to say that? How could she? Of course, she has the right to say it, if she meant it. It is always right to say what is right, even when that means that you have to admit that you did wrong. But Ms. Flowers was not content to leave it there. Reading between the lines, one can see that she was arguing that Bill Clinton was wrong, too. And still is, if the allegations raised about any number of women prove true.

But she was not content to leave well enough alone even there. She went a step further. A step not many Americans have been shrewd enough to take in recent years. She insisted that the president of the United States is a role model, whether he means to be or not. Or whether a large percentage of Americans think he needs to be one or not. By nature of the office he sought to win with all of his charm and charisma, Bill Clinton is a role model for all Americans. Especially for "the children."

Gennifer Flowers was not alone in that opinion. Almost alone (if you go by the soaring approval polls), but not quite. Mike Barnicle, a columnist for the *Boston Globe,* forecast the danger of sticking our heads in the sand and refusing to recognize that the president of the United States is a role model for "the children":

> [I]t struck me that if we employed the logic of these preposterous people who claim Clinton's relationship

with his intern is none of our business... I mean, if
character and judgment aren't any big priority in a
president, why torture our own children about their
importance?...

So what do we tell them about the fog of fibs, the
constant evasion of truth, and the complete lack of
explanation from a president who has built a career by
leaning on polls and relying on charm to distance
himself from complete answers to legitimate
questions? That if you learn to lie well enough, you,
too, can go to the White House?[8]

Even Michael Kinsley, the card-carrying liberal from the
left coast, agreed that character matters in politicians
because they have set themselves up as role models.
Surprised? Read this. You will be left speechless:

The one thing I would say is that wherever you draw
that line, you draw it differently for a politician, who
has put him or herself forward, asking for your
approval, and also, in general, has presented a picture
of him or herself as a traditional family person and
therefore has put their privacy in play, I think.[9]

Not everyone agrees with that perspective. Many people
seem to think that all that matters is whether the economy
is sound and Saddam is kept in check. If the president can
tackle those affairs of state, he can have all of the other
kinds of affairs he wants, these folks would argue. His
"affairs" are his affair, so to speak.

This approach was personified by Bob Guccione. If you

were Bill Clinton (embroiled in a sex scandal), how would you like to have the publisher of *Penthouse* come to your defense? With friends like that, who needs a right-wing conspiracy, right? But Guccione did stand up for Clinton, publicly. "The president's private life should be his own. I don't think we have any right to invade it."[10] Privately, however, he tried to do just that. He approached Monica Lewinsky with $2 million for a "tell-all" partial-nude photo shoot. How's that for a schizophrenic vote of confidence for "the Animal House President?"[11] — Maureen Dowd's caricature of Clinton, believe it or not.

This "character doesn't matter" argument is the Susan B. Anthony approach to political morality. This famed mother-of-all-feminists argued, "If a man's public record be a clear one, if he has kept his pledges before the world, I do not inquire what his private life may have been."[12] Harry Truman didn't buy that kind of fuzzy logic. As a Democrat and one of Mr. Clinton's preferred presidential role models, Truman took pains to remind the voting public (and Mr. Clinton, if he had his ears on) that the president of the United States is a role model:

> I've said before, the President is the only person in the government who represents the whole people... and when there's a moral issue involved, the President has to be the moral leader of the country.[13]

In contrast to Mr. Truman, Alan Lichtman, a historian

who seems to know a lot about presidential sex lives, thinks the rest of us are on "a need to know basis" only. He seemed proud of the new sophistication of the American people when he voiced his vote for the postmodern code of conduct:

> Well, I certainly think when it comes to sexual alleg-
> ations, the public, at least, for this president and for
> other presidents as well, is willing to have a pretty high
> discount factor for the president's personal life. It
> doesn't mean character doesn't count. I think it does.
> But I think they're judging character more in terms of
> the conduct of the office as opposed to the personal
> conduct of the individual....
>
> And I think that what you often get lost in is the
> difference between purely personal behavior and the
> public conduct of a president. You can't totally
> separate the two, but they can often get blurred.[14]

Ah, but, Mr. Lichtman, can you really separate the two? Doesn't the conduct of the office-holder and the conduct of the office do more than blur around the edges? Doesn't the judgment that the president displays in his private affairs (pardon the possible double entendre) offer a central clue to the kind of judgment he exercises in affairs of state? Two days after the Fornigate scandal broke reporter Steve Roberts was a guest on CNN's "Talkback Live." He made an excellent point about how private and public character not only blur but blend together:

> If we didn't cover Bill Clinton in this way, don't you

have a right to know this element of Bill Clinton's character? Doesn't that directly affect his judgment as a president? This is not just about scandal, and it's not just about sex. It's about his judgment.

And, you know, there are an awful lot of Democrats today in this town saying, "Could he possibly have been that stupid?" Well, don't you deserve to know whether he was that stupid or not?[15]

In other words, don't we have a right to know whether we have "a government headed by a kind of Joey Buttafucco with Ivy League polish,"[16] to borrow from Mike Barnicle's caricature of Mr. Clinton? Doesn't his flawed judgment in the Lewinsky affair or the Willey incident make a strong statement about the man, no matter what the state of the economy might be? Think not? Then think again, Barnicle argued:

> Now, frustrated and angered by his inability to issue a flat-out denial devoid of linguistic tricks, the crowd lives with the uneasy knowledge that they have a terribly flawed man in the White House whom they trust with the economy but not with their own daughters.[17]

Even some hard-core liberals have been forced to agree with Barnicle's brand of logic. One of them, Tavis Smiley, the author of *Hard Left: Straight Talk About the Wrongs of the Right*, can't possibly be lumped into some vague right-wing conspiracy. But, Smiley admitted on *CNN's* "Talk-Back Live":

> But I will give you this. I'll be the first to admit... that if these charges that have been levied against President Clinton turn out to be true.... If the president did these things, he ought to be dealt with and dealt with severely.[18]

Oh my! Did Mr. Smiley really mean to say that? Is it fair to say that Bill Clinton is accountable to the American people for his private affairs? Does it matter if the president behaves badly in private as long as he produces for the public good? Or think of it this way: Do we really care if we have presidential men behaving badly?

Tavis Smiley seems to think so. After all, Mr. Clinton chose to be elected to a public post. As Gertrude Himmelfarb argued:

> President Clinton has a good deal to answer for, not only for his behavior, if the accusations are substantiated, but in making the public his accomplice—putting it on trial and exposing its moral equivocations. The president's legacy, some now say, will be the memory of a scandal-ridden administration. The public's legacy will be a further vulgarization and demoralization of society.[19]

Ah, there it is: the legacy question. Pundits of every political stripe have been kicking around the question, "What will President Clinton's legacy be?" Will he get full credit for balancing the federal budget? Or will he get only partial credit because the Republicans twisted his arm to get that feat accomplished? Will he get credit for a great economy? Or will Alan Greenspan get most of the "atta-boys"? It has been comical to watch this meaningless debate.

Why? Because there has been no question for several years that not long after the last approval rating has been cited for the Clinton presidency, his legacy would be plain for all to see. It will be as plain as, some would say, the nose on his face. Character matters. That will be the Clinton legacy. How a president conducts himself in his private affairs does shape his conduct in affairs of state. His judgment governs both the country and the individual man. George Will was right when he wrote:

> Years hence, when Clinton's presidency is just a faint memory... it will be studied as a demonstration of how a president's character and nonpublic behavior (behavior unrelated to policies) can work institutional—even, in a sense, constitutional—change in the office.[20]

But you can hear the inevitable protest that will be raised to the character question, can't you? You might have already raised it yourself. "What about President Kennedy? Didn't he engage in his own series of presidential sexcapades?" the argument runs. "But everyone thinks that he was a great president. So, if character matters, how do you explain that apparent contradiction?" Good questions!

Do you believe this?

I think that if you look at the history of the presidency, a lot of these kinds of things have happened. There were a lot of rumors about John F. Kennedy having affairs, and it was never really mentioned that he should be impeached or any of those things.

—FORMER INTERN IN
BILL CLINTON'S WHITE HOUSE

But John F. Kennedy Did It!

Nobody asks better questions than nationally syndicated columnist Mona Charen. But even she outdid herself when she posed this rhetorical question: "Are the American people so cynical or so decadent that they are willing to tolerate acts by a president that NBC refused to condone in a sportscaster, provided the economy is humming?" Ah, yes. That was the question of the everlasting Lewinsky news cycle. Are the American people now prepared to accept Marv Albert as their next president, bite marks and all?

Not long after the allegations about Monica Lewinsky surfaced, pundits appeared on talk shows to begin to manipulate public opinion. How did they do it? By pointing out that other presidents had their own sexual flings. Plenty of other presidents were as guilty as Mr. Clinton, they suggested. What he was alleged to have done might be worse by degree than most (though clearly not in the case of John Kennedy), but what are a few degrees of separation among fellow presidents? These pundits did not argue that every president has done it. But they insinuated that enough have done it to whitewash President Clinton's dirty deeds. Estimates run as high as 13 out of 42 presidents that have cheated on their wives.[21] On its face, this appears to be an intimidating argument.

To compound the problem, Grover Cleveland, when he was confronted with a sex scandal of his own, muttered for the public record, "I don't think the American people want a gelding in the White House."[22] This brash response by one ex-president has been used to help exonerate the current occupant of the Oval Office. It is designed to intimidate those who find the president's behavior distasteful, but who don't want to appear too puritanical. This historical spin runs something like this:

Thomas Jefferson may have done it. Andrew Jackson was accused of doing it. We know that Grover Cleveland and Warren Harding did it. FDR did it with maybe only one woman. Jack Kennedy did it with most of the women on the Atlantic seaboard.

What these men have in common—very common, you might say—is that they bedded women not their wives.[23]

One other world-class womanizer and former president was left out of this list of promiscuous presidents: Lyndon Johnson. When told of JFK's womanizing, Johnson is reported to have bragged, "G___ D___ it, I had more women by accident than he ever had by design!"[24] His private boast gave new meaning to the once popular campaign slogan, "All the way with LBJ!" Johnson was proud of using women as pawns for his personal pleasure, and callous to the pain he inflicted on his dear wife. During an interview after her husband died, Lady Bird Johnson was asked about her husband's reputation with the ladies. She gallantly tried to put the best face on her husband's infidelity. "My husband loved people. All people. And half the people in the world were women," Lady Bird commented demurely. "You don't think I could have kept my husband away from half the people?" But at that point the pretense gave way to her pain. Lady Bird's eyes clouded with tears, and she added, "He loved me. I know he only loved me."[25]

So, yes! It is true. Other presidents have cheated on their wives. So what? This line of argument boils down to nothing more than an Oval Office reissue of the old 1960's excuse, "But everybody's doin' it!" As one very sensible woman asked, "Does that mean we should excuse Bill Clinton's billy-goat behavior because he's in good historical company?"[26]

It is not fair when some wag wanders into your living room by way of the local newspaper and claims "America has condoned such activity throughout history."[27] Americans have not condoned this kind of behavior in their presidents in the past. They have been kept ignorant of it (except in the case of Grover Cleveland). Even Alan Lichtman had to admit regarding the Clinton sex scandal, "Well, it's the first time a scandal involving allegations of sex [has] exploded on a sitting president."[28]

Consider, too, that this is not a simple case of adultery that is alleged regarding Bill Clinton. Women who have accommodated Bill Clinton or have been accosted by him keep popping out of the woodwork. There is a terrifying pattern of infidelity here. Bill Clinton doesn't love women. He uses them, and then trashes them like used Kleenexes. This is a flagrant abuse of power. Suzanne Fields hit the nail on the head:

> If the allegations of Paula Jones and Monica Lewinsky are true, there's a major difference in the romps of Mr.

Clinton and the bedtime adventures of his predeces-
sors.[29]

Then what are we to think? If other presidents cheated on
their wives, should we ignore the fact that President
Clinton has allegedly cheated on his wife again, and
again, and again? Should we apply Alan Richtman's logic
and conclude that what was good enough for JFK is good
enough for WJC?

> For example, with all the revelations that have come
> out about fairly substantial evidence about affairs being
> conducted by John Kennedy, his esteem in the eyes of
> the public has not plummeted. He still remains a figure
> of high esteem because of the public record.[30]

Ah, but Mr. Richtman, will John Kennedy be judged with
"high esteem" by future generations that will not be
emotionally involved with artificial images of "Camelot"?
Will those who do not remember what they were doing
when they heard that JFK was assassinated have a vested
interest in keeping the fiction alive? Or will they be more
enchanted by *The Dark Side of Camelot,* as Seymour
Hersh depicted the Kennedy years? Won't images of the
president regularly entertaining prostitutes for his own
pleasure discolor those camera-ready images of John
Kennedy, family man?

Besides, the public-at-large didn't know about
Kennedy's womanizing. Rumors about his paramours

floated discreetly in certain circles in Washington and in Hollywood. But those of us in "fly-over country" were judged to be too naïve to handle this sensitive information. But suppose that Kennedy's sexcapades had become public knowledge back then? Would he still have been lauded as a family man, or celebrated as a folk hero today?

Do you think that the American public in 1963 would have turned a deaf ear if they had known that the president made it a practice to skinny-dip in the pool at lunch time with two young women that "all the president's men" nicknamed Fiddle and Faddle? Would the average American have turned over and yawned to allegations that the president of the United States was having hookers brought to his hotel room or into 1600 Pennsylvania Avenue itself?

Do you honestly think that Americans would have tolerated knowing that JFK shared Judith Exner with mob boss Sam Giancana? Or that he used her as a conduit for information flowing to and from Giancana? Is it likely that Americans who were living under the shadow of a nuclear winter would have been pleased to hear that the president was having an affair with an East German spy?

Let's be honest. If John F. Kennedy had not been assassinated by a bullet in November of 1963, he might have been assassinated by a sex scandal by November of 1964. His reckless behavior could have blown the image of Camelot to kingdom come:

Given the facts now available, it is clear that Kennedy abused his high position for personal self-gratification. His reckless liaisons with women and mobsters were irresponsible, dangerous, and demeaning to the office of the chief executive. They were irresponsible because of the enormous potential for scandal and blackmail they posed. Any number of women, gangsters, intelligence agents, and journalists might have used their knowledge of Kennedy's sexual meandering to force concessions from the office of the president.[31]

Not even *Washington Post* columnist David Broder could be pacified by efforts to excuse Bill Clinton's nasty behavior by comparing it to President Kennedy's sexcapades. With a strong hint of disgust in every keystroke, Broder reflected on JFK as "the man we belatedly learned carried on a variety of reckless assignations inside and outside the White House."[32]

Does anybody hope to seriously propose that we make John Kennedy's reckless behavior the standard for all future presidents? Shouldn't we, instead, examine the character deficiencies of President Kennedy, as Thomas Reeves urged us to do in his brilliant analysis, *A Question of Character?* In it he presented to the country this stinging indictment of JFK's character (or lack thereof):

Beneath the surface, however, Jack was pragmatic to the point of amorality; his sole standard seemed to be political expediency. Gifted with good looks, youth, and wealth, he was often, in his personal life, reckless, vain, selfish, petty, and lecherous. Jack's character... lacked a moral center, a reference point that went beyond self-aggrandizement.[33]

Remember, the public had no idea what Kennedy was doing behind closed doors. But for those who did know, it became a joke, and so did the presidency.

Kennedy's adultery also demeaned the presidency. Many people in Washington, Hollywood, and elsewhere made the man the butt of jokes and gossip which surely lowered their, and others', respect for the nation's highest office.[34]

Today, the American people are very much aware of what Bill Clinton has been doing behind closed doors. We know more than any of us care to know. How much more have the actions of this president demeaned "the nation's highest office"?

It isn't our business, people say, whether the president has had an affair. But why is it too much to ask a man to exercise personal restraint if he chooses to seek the highest office in the land? If it is someone who has a past and has put that past behind him or her, the American people could tolerate that. But why should "we the people" tolerate a man or woman who is not willing to make some personal sacrifices to earn the right to lead. It isn't a matter of looking for perfect men or women to serve the nation. But shouldn't we be allowed to weed out men or women whose imperfections make them unfit to lead by example? President Kennedy was guilty of using women as pawns for his personal pleasure. It will prove to be a dark blot on his legacy. The same holds true for President Clinton. Let's hope that "we the people" will never tolerate another president who abuses his power to use women, or uses his power to abuse women.

Early in the 21st century, Seymour Hersh's verdict on John F. Kennedy will become the verdict of historians. They will be harsh in reviewing "the dark side" of Kennedy's Camelot. His reckless *personal* behavior led to reckless *official* behavior. Those 1,000 days of Camelot, the glorious celebration of the Kennedy years, was as much a work of fiction as the Camelot of King Arthur. It was a myth. Future historians will not make excuses for Kennedy as so many are willing to do even now. Those students of history will not have the emotional baggage of Kennedy's assassination to cloud their senses.

Unfortunately, the verdict on Bill Clinton will be just as severe. His reckless personal behavior has translated into reckless official deeds—not the least of which was allowing money to flow from Red China into the coffers of the Democratic Party through his friends Charlie Trie and John Huang. Nobody can make that charge stick right now. But future historians will put two and two together and not come up with zero. Whether he is ever held accountable in a court of law, Bill Clinton will be convicted by the court of public opinion not long after we have crossed his bridge to the 21st century—if not before.

If Hillary Doesn't Care, Why Should We?

Sometimes we don't give television audiences enough credit. Especially a "live" audience. But a young man who got his 15 seconds of fame on CNN's "Talk-Back Live" made the most of his moment in the spotlight. He had enough sense to figure out what many of the pundits have yet to discover: Bill Clinton has a tough time keeping his word to anyone. "But how can we trust his oath to the country," he asked, "if we don't know if he can stay true to his wife?" [35] In other words, if he cheats on his wife, how do we know he won't cheat on America?

What a great question! If the president can't be trusted to keep a vow to one person, how can he be trusted to keep his oath to 270 million others? Shame on the president for violating his vow to his wife! But shame on the rest of us for failing to get the connection. Give that young man a Pulitzer for asking a question most reporters never understood to be relevant.

No doubt the Lewinsky scandal has raised questions that may never be answered to everybody's satisfaction. But David Maraniss, the "official" unofficial biographer of Bill Clinton, gave voice to the questions that most people would have loved to ask Hillary after the Lewinsky affair broke:

> What would she do, and why would she do it? Would this be one sex story too many for her to tolerate? Would she pack up and leave? Would she recede from public view in a state of depression, or would she take the lead on her husband's behalf?[36]

Publicly, she has stood by her husband, assuring the public that she believed his denials. Privately, according to one White House "deep throat," the news hit the First Lady hard. On the day that the story broke Hillary took a train to Baltimore for a speaking engagement. President Clinton called her on her cell phone three times during that trip. Her assistant, who had the cell phone, answered all three calls. But Hillary refused to speak to Bill.

A couple of days later, she learned that her husband had given Monica Lewinsky a copy of Walt Whitman's *Leaves of Grass*. She was visibly shaken by the news. "He gave me the same book after our second date," she remarked. Bill didn't feel her pain. She felt her own pain.

For Hillary, dealing with the aftershocks of her playboy husband is nothing new. David Maraniss insists that Hillary knew what she was up against before she married him. When she first moved to Arkansas Bill was caught up in the heat of a congressional campaign. But he was "in heat" in another sense, too. He was tramping around northwest Arkansas, Maraniss said, "and he had girlfriends in several towns." One of those girls turned out to be the girlfriend of one of Clinton's campaign workers. There were some close calls, Maraniss noted:

> Paul Fray, the campaign coordinator, said he and his wife were often put in the position of shooing an Arkansas woman out the back door when Hillary was coming in the front.[37]

Most Americans know in their heart of hearts that Bill Clinton is a philanderer, a womanizer. Though they may deny it privately, people flaunt this belief, publicly. Witness the national laugh lines emanating from David Letterman on the right coast to Jay Leno on the left coast. Audiences laugh at what they know is true to life. Jokes about Mr. Clinton's sexual antics resonate even in fly-over country. But while America laughs out loud, does Hillary cry inside?

We may never see Hillary's pain. For the cameras she stands by her man. In her first formal television interview after the Lewinsky scandal broke, Hillary came out swinging. On NBC's *Today Show* she blamed the scandal on a "vast right-wing conspiracy." But she also tried to set the record straight about the First Marriage. "The only two people who count in any marriage are the two people that are in it," she lectured Matt Lauer. "We know everything there is to know about each other, and we understand and accept and love each other."[38] Somehow that sounds more cold and calculating than warm and loving.

One of the editors of *The Nation* magazine, a lofty liberal rag, interpreted Hillary's suggestion that the two people in a marriage are the only ones who know what is going on as "almost a tacit comment on that they may have an arrangement."[39] Is the Clinton marriage on the up-and-up? Are they the loving couple they have publicly tried to portray themselves to be? Was that photo-op of the First Couple dancing romantically on the beach in swim-suits on their Christmas vacation the real thing? Or was that staged, knowing that their marriage was about to be tested on the rocks aboard *Lady Monica?* Where does the truth lie?

One F.O.B. (Friend of Bill) gushed, "He loves her as much as he is capable of loving any woman. I think she knows that."[40] Lovely! What kind of ringing endorsement is that? He loves her as much as he loves any woman. Swell! A friend of the First Lady did a little better than that. She explained, "I think she's goofy about him."[41] Maybe some women believe that. But there are many women who would accept only one-third of that explanation: "She's goofy!" Noemie Emery gave voice to that sentiment when she described Hillary as "the most humiliated woman in the world."[42]

A New York therapist put the First Couple on his couch, metaphorically speaking, and offered this analysis of their relationship:

> It's more along a European model of a marriage. Maybe she understands that it's not her job to control him, that this is his problem, his sickness, and it won't change, but at the end of the day, she's the one he comes home to.[43]

A different kind of analyst offered his own take on the First Marriage. Political consultant Dick Morris, a former F.O.B., went public with some dirty laundry. On the air with talk radio jockeys from KABC in Los Angeles he speculated:

> None of what I'm about to say is necessarily a fact. I don't know it. But let's assume, OK, that his sexual

relationship with Hillary is not all that it's supposed to be. Let's assume that some of the allegations that Hillary sometimes not necessarily being into regular sex with men might be true.

Let's assume that this is a guy who has been sexually active for a long time and then got in as president and he'd have to shut himself down. You would then expect a variety of things which would be quasi-sexual in nature but which would fall short of it.

Phone sex would be one of them, fantasies might be one of them, a close emotional relationship with a young person might be one of them. Those all could be real things without actually committing adultery....[44]

Keep in mind that Dick Morris is an expert when it comes to adultery. If it takes one to know one, then Morris' take on the president and First Lady might need to be taken more seriously.

While trying to define Hillary's "mystique," Barbara Lippert speculated in the *New Yorker Magazine* that the First Lady may have made her own pact with the devil. "She has made the kind of Faustian bargain that mere mortals not so in control of their ambitions and emotions just can't fathom."[45] If you buy that, it is very difficult to imagine Hillary ever plucking petals from a daisy, musing, "He loves me, he loves me not...."

Not to be outdone by the *New Yorker,* the *New Republic* joined in the chorus of left-swingers who deplored the state of the union in the First Marriage. Bemoaning the "hypocrisy of Hillaryism," Barbara Talbot castigated the First Lady:

> So the bargain she seems to have made—to put up with the humiliations of marriage to an apparently indefatigable womanizer in exchange for a share of his power —seems, increasingly, like just that: a bargain, an unidealistic and demeaning deal that allows her to attain public authority at the cost of her own dignity.[46]

This talk of a deal, an arrangement between the First Couple, conjures up an old image. Do you remember Monty Hall's old game show, "Let's Make A Deal"? Picture Hillary as one of the contestants in the audience. With half-naked bimbos erupting from Door #1, Door #2, and Door #3, Hillary stands resolute in her clown costume. She has made up her mind. No, she will not trade in her husband. She will take what is in the envelope: an agreement to wield greater power in exchange for her silence. For Hillary, it seems, silence is a golden opportunity.

Maureen Dowd agrees. She appears to believe that Hillary learned "the art of the deal" at Donald Trump's knee. With undisguised contempt for what she perceived as the First Couple's hypocrisy, she sniped, "Hillary Clinton knows her husband is a hound dog. She knew it before she married him. But they have their deal."[47]

Is it a good deal for the country, you may wonder?

Some feminists like Susan Estrich have suggested that

it is all right for women to trade sex to gain power. (Or in Hillary's case, to trade the loss of sex.) Margaret Talbot and the *New Republic* did not see it that way. Ms. Talbot accused Hillary of feeding her husband's addiction in a sick co-dependent relationship. Hillary standing by her man, Talbot insisted:

> . . . leaves us with the image of a wife who, to borrow from the therapeutic language to which the Clintons sometimes repair, seeks to "empower" herself through "enabling" her husband.[48]

Or worse still, Talbot asserts, Bill Clinton "is a man who did not have enough respect for his wife, or concern for 'women's issues'... to keep his zipper up." Not to let Hillary off the hook, Talbot added, "And his wife is his accomplice."[49] This does not leave Hillary looking like the poor little innocent wife. She has been reduced to a pathetic figure seduced by the trappings of power.

While many women still stand by President Clinton, other women have been troubled by the image of Hillary standing by her man. Barbara Ehrenreich is one of those. She donated a piece of her mind to Hillary that she will never be able to retrieve:

> Someone needs to tell this woman that the first time a wife stands up for an allegedly adulterous husband, everyone think she's a saint. The second or third time, though, she begins to look disturbingly complicit.[50]

But the Tammy Wynette role has even worse implications for Hillary. As Margaret Talbot alerted readers of the *New Republic*, Hillary has betrayed the gains that women have made against old-fashioned stereotypes:

> Standing by her man has also, of course, meant colluding in a damage-control campaign that traffics in some rather unsavory stereotypes about women. Gennifer Flowers was lying because she was a tramp; Paula Jones was lying because she was trailer-trash; Monica Lewinsky is lying because she is "flighty, flirtatious, prone to exaggeration," as National Public Radio correspondent Mara Liasson characterized the off-the-record picture of the former intern that mysteriously leaked from the White House this week. That, it seems, is Bill Clinton's m.o.: hit on them and then humiliate them.[51]

By becoming Bill's "public defender, lashing out at his 'enemies,'" Hillary has shrunk "to the seemingly masochistic role of First Nanny."[52] It is a steep drop from First Feminist to First Nanny. According to the *New Republic*, this hypocrisy stripped Hillary of her right to be a role model for women. Ms. Talbot raged:

> [I]t seems harder than ever to scrunch our eyes shut and construe Hillary Clinton as a feminist icon, a role model for young women of talent and ambition.[53]

A close friend of the Clinton's, when asked why Hillary does not walk away, muttered, "They do not have the kind of marriage you and I have."[54] Ah, yes! This is the first postmodern "First Marriage." It does not appear to be an affair of love. This marriage appears to be an affair of state. Cynics wonder whether this First Marriage will end in the first divorce of a former First Couple:

> Clinton-haters and even some supporters wonder whether the marriage will end with the presidency.... As long as they're in the limelight, their turbulent partnership seems certain to endure—for better or worse. That's because they see themselves in almost Messianic terms, as great leaders who have a mission to fulfill.[55]

Many years ago back in Arkansas, Hillary wondered out loud to a friend, "I wonder how history is going to note our marriage."[56] Now that should prove to be an interesting question! How will historians judge the Clinton marriage? Not the court of public opinion. Not the opinion polls. Rather the historians who do not have to prove their perspective in a court of law. What verdict will they hand down about the first postmodern First Marriage?

One of the glib responses to the Lewinsky scandal was the oft-expressed sentiment: If Hillary doesn't care, why should we? Why do the people who say that assume that Hillary doesn't care? How do they know? How do they know what Hillary feels about all of this? While "we the people" joke out loud over Bill's peccadilloes in offices all over the land, Hillary might not be laughing. Why do pundits presume to know how Hillary feels?

If Hillary doesn't care about her husband's infidelities, that's her problem. Many people do care. I suspect, if you have read this far, you do! If Hillary doesn't care, that says more about her than we may care to know. If we don't care about his infidelities, that says more about us than we dare to know. If the Clintons have made peace about their postmodern First Marriage, that is between them. If "we the people" endorse their postmodern arrangement, that is far more troubling. God help us, if that is the case. But will He?

Do you believe this?

SPEAKING OF PAULA JONES,
A WOMAN FROM COLUMBUS, OHIO, WROTE:
*"Jones has received more than enough celebrity and
attention to compensate her fairly for any harm
she may have suffered from Clinton."*[57]

Where Is N.O.W. Now?

"As women and lawyers we must never again shy from raising our voices against sexual harassment," demanded one ardent feminist in defense of Anita Hill. "All women who care about equality of opportunity—about integrity and morality in the workplace—are in Professor Hill's debt."[58]

Who was that articulate defender of Anita Hill, and what does she think of the sexual harassment allegations lodged against Bill Clinton by both Paula Jones and Kathleen Willey? (After all, the charges against Clarence Thomas were never more than allegations. They were never proven.) This strident defender of Ms. Hill was none other than "our First Feminist,"[59] Hillary Rodham Clinton. You be the judge. Do you think that she has shied away from raising her voice against sexual harassment on behalf of Paula Jones and Kathleen Willey?

Then, too, was she the only one? Pat Schroeder was one of more than a half dozen congresswomen who marched into the Senate chamber to protest against Clarence Thomas. But Schroeder saw no need to lodge a similar protest against Clinton for fooling around with a White House intern. "Wasn't she an adult?" she asked. "Wasn't she of age?" Besides, "if Clinton was calling women into the Oval Office and then attacking them," she added, "I think you would see a very different response, but that's not the allegation."[60] But, Ms. Schroeder, that *is* the allegation against the president in the case of Kathleen Willey. So, where is that "very different response" you alluded to?

Nita Lowey, who joined Schroeder in that picturesque march on Washington's "boys will be boys club," also refused to lodge a similar protest against Clinton:

> I'm going to continue to fight for women to have a fair opportunity to get a fair hearing. If a woman feels victimized in the workplace, she should be able to seek redress. But that isn't the case here.[61]

Oh, isn't it, Ms. Lowey? What about Kathleen Willey, who

has begrudgingly testified to being sexually harassed by the president? When asked that question, Lowey dodged the bullet by shrieking, "This is a rumor! I don't like to deal with speculation." One wonders if she would dodge that bullet for a Republican president.

Other feminists have joined ranks in this conspiracy of silence. Gloria Steinem, who had a physiological case of laryngitis when the Lewinsky scandal broke, seemed to acquire situational laryngitis when she finally was capable of speaking out. "Do I wish that all this turns out to be false?" she asked a *New York Times* reporter. "Yes, deeply I wish that. But I am not blameless. How can I require a leader to be blameless?"[62] Pardon me, Ms. Steinem. Did you feel the same way about Senator Bob Packwood or Clarence Thomas? Were you willing to excuse their foibles because you have your own foibles? Surely Ms. Steinem can do better than that!

Apparently, Patricia Ireland, the President of N.O.W., couldn't. When allegations surfaced about Bob Packwood, Ms. Ireland declared war. "This has to be a heads-up for men in power," she demanded. "You can't treat women as the spoils of power."[63] Power can't be exploited for pleasure, she insisted.

Does that mean that Patricia was troubled by allegations that President Clinton had exploited his power and position with a subordinate who was on the bottom of the White House food chain? Hardly! When confronted with Bill Clinton's pattern of womanizing, Ms. Ireland blinked. "If there is a pattern, it appears to be a pattern of consensual sex."[64] Has N.O.W. been seduced by Clinton's charisma and reduced to the "National Organization for Womanizers"?[65]

Unfortunately, the president of the National Abortion Rights Action League (NARAL) didn't fare any better. "Until we know the facts, the real facts of what happened," said Kate Michelman, "it's not a good idea to speculate on anything." One wonders whether she would exercise the same patience in waiting for "the facts" if this were a Republican who was charged with being an "Oval Office Romeo"?[66]

When charges were swirling around Bob Packwood's head, Michelman flushed him, viewing his behavior as "an egregious violation of his commitment to women's issues."[67] But with similar charges swirling around Bill Clinton's waist, she praised him for demonstrating "the courage of his convictions" on women's issues.[68] Did she intend that to be a joke, or did it just come off funny?

Maybe it is time for the Ms. Steinems, Ms. Irelands, Ms. Michelmans, and Ms. Clintons of the world to take inventory. They would do well to give an honest answer to the question raised by Patricia Ireland during the Packwood scandal. As an explanation for her refusal to stand by Packwood despite his stands for women's issues, Ireland asked, "Can we be bought? And, if so, how cheap?"[69] Apparently, in Bill Clinton's "meat market," feminists are quite cheap.

Thank goodness that when all the professional feminists lost their tongues, Ellen Goodman was willing to exercise hers. As a co-conspirator in feminist causes, Ms. Goodman broke with the conspiracy of silence engaged in by the sisterhood. She confessed to being uncomfortable when it came to having to be "pro-choice" for Clinton:

> We are being asked which we would rather have: A man who is faithful to his wife but betrays the policy aspirations of women? Or a philanderer who "gets it" on child care, education, Medicare? Isn't there another multiple choice?[70]

Ms. Goodman may not have bowled over her readers with answers to those questions or others, but she dished out some exquisite questions:

> Why haven't the soccer moms decided to throw Clinton out of the (White) House? Why are the Democratic women pols who shot off their mouths about Clarence Thomas, holding their tongues about Bill? And, above all, why aren't feminists who put sexual harassment on the office bulletin board standing by their Monica?[71]

Or Kathleen? Or Paula? Or, who knows the names of how many others—or dozens of others—if the rumors about hundreds of women are true?

Maureen Dowd was equally troubled by the vow of silence taken by the N.O.W. Sisterhood. She cited their entire dubious track record:

> They were not in full throat when James Carville suggested Paula Jones was trailer trash, when Bob Bennett compared Paula Jones to a dog, when Clintonites wrote up talking points to discredit Kathleen Willey, and when the Clinton attack team roughed up Ms. Lewinsky.... Funny, I thought feminism was devised to root out all those "he's a stud, she's a slut" double standards.[72]

But it wasn't just the conduct of the male Clinton goon squad that bothered Ms. Dowd. It was the consent of the "First Feminist" and her feminist co-conspirators in Congress that troubled her as much or more: It is probably just a matter of moments before we hear that Ms. Lewinsky is a little nutty and a little slutty....

> The feminist icon in the White House doesn't flinch at smearing these women, even when she suspects they're telling the truth, because she feels they're instruments of a conspiracy....
>
> Ms. Lewinsky must die so that the women of America can have better child care, longer maternity stays, toll-free domestic violence hot lines and bustling mutual funds.
>
> Mrs. Clinton knows she can count on the complicity of feminists and Democratic women in Congress. They accept the trade-off in letting a few women be debased

so that they can get more day-care centers.[73]

"Isn't that hypocritical?" you might be tempted to ask. Of course it is. As Gwen Rickardson wrote in a *USA Today* editorial, "Those who were so zealous to 'uncloak' Thomas are now, hypocritically, putting the brakes on 'uncloaking' Clinton."[74] As we approach Bill Clinton's "bridge to the 21st century" at warp speed, tolerance is America's only virtue and hypocrisy is America's only vice. But even by those limited postmodern standards of right and wrong, feminists and their ideology have flunked the test. They have allowed Bill Clinton to proposition them on a public street, and now the vice squad must haul them in and charge them with hypocrisy.

This deafening silence from the professional feminists puts the finger on another great weakness in America's postmodern moral code—or lack thereof. There are no fixed standards—no absolutes—that apply in all cases at all times. When Clarence Thomas had allegations of sexual harassment thrown his way, he was fair game because he was too conservative to dance to the feminists' tune. Those allegations suggested that Thomas may have talked dirty to Anita Hill, but he did not touch her or expose himself to her. However, Bill Clinton has been charged with exposing himself to Paula Jones and fondling Kathleen Willey. But Mr. Clinton has not missed a step in dancing the feminist jig. So the feminists have not come to the defense of Ms. Jones or Ms. Willey. They are reluctant to jettison Bill Clinton, as Barbara Ehrenreich suggested, "just because he might have a little problem keeping his fly zipped up."[75]

The following letter-to-the-editor was written in August 1996—not January 1998. This woman was right to speak out then. She deserves to speak out now:

"Support for Clinton by Women Unfathomable"

As a woman, I am completely astounded and disgusted when I see the polling information that shows that the majority of women support Bill Clinton.

Why would women support a man who treats our gender with such disrespect? With every fiber of my being, I cannot understand this. He has exhibited this blatant lack of respect for his wife, his daughter and women in general by his repeated immoral and adulterous actions.

I would be ashamed to have Bill Clinton as a husband, a father or a son, and I am definitely ashamed to have him as president of the United States of America.[76]

Mr. Clinton may be a sexual predator, devouring every woman in his path, but feminists will stand by their man.

As long as he favors a woman's "reproductive rights" he can have the right to any woman he wants. As Kate O'Beirne put it, "Feminists just don't get it: they will stand by their man, even when he's walking all over them."[77] In the process their postmodern Monopoly game has been trampled in the dust.

Do you believe this?
It's like he's accused of robbing a bank...
and he gets up there and says, "Absolutely not.
Those allegations are untrue. I did not rob a bank."
Later on, when he gets caught, he tells us,
"You don't understand. I didn't lie. I never robbed
a bank. It was a savings and loan."[78]

Those Irksome "Non-Denial Denials"

"**P**lainly, he's lying. Plainly, he did it."

Oh, that must be another one of those right-wing fanatics sounding off. Is that what you think? Hardly! That was comedian Bill Maher on *Politically Incorrect,* the trash-talk show that he hosts. He was reacting to allegations about the new sex scandal in the White House. But Maher was not upset with the president. He was frustrated with the American people who were stupid enough to think that lying is a big deal. He explained:

> What do you think about this naíve belief that this country seems to have about that you have to tell the truth all the time? Isn't this silly and naíve? I mean, don't we all lie sometimes? And is that really the mark of morality? Isn't sometimes a mistruth a sign of doing something nice for someone? Are we all really supposed to tell the truth all the time?[79]

What was Maher's point? Essentially, he was saying—whether he understood it or not—"Why is it important that we be able to trust the president of the United States to tell the truth? Why is that a big deal? Doesn't everybody lie? Why should the president be held to a higher standard than we hold ourselves to?" It was an exquisite snapshot of a postmodern approach to morality. "Why do we need standards for anybody, let alone the president?" a thoroughly postmodern Millie would argue.

Are you comfortable with that brand of logic? Is that acceptable to you? It certainly didn't fly with David Broder. Nobody would ever think to accuse Broder of being part of some "vast right-wing conspiracy." He has never been shy in spouting liberal notions. But after this recent Fornigate scandal broke, Broder surprised everyone with an editorial that accused Presidents Kennedy and Clinton of "reckless" behavior. Charging that "This nation deserves better of its leaders," Broder referred to Clinton's alleged behavior as "sexual prowling" and "tomcatting."

Further, Broder suggested that Clinton has acted "to camouflage the truth." He wrote:

> But to believe Clinton's denials, one must once again presume that a succession of women over a period of two decades have concocted tales of his sexual prowling and invented charges that he told them how to camouflage the truth. [80]

Broder was troubled by what he described as the "clipped, strained non-answer answers" that Clinton sputtered, "all the while insisting that he is cooperating with the investigation of his actions." [81]

Yes, you remember those "strained" non-denial denials, don't you. "There is not a sexual relationship," he told Jim Lehrer. Wouldn't you have loved to hear Lehrer fire back, "But Mr. President, nobody is suggesting that there still *is* a sexual relationship. But many people would like to ask you, 'Did you and Ms. Lewinsky *ever* have a sexual relationship?'"

But then, as we later discovered, that question might not have achieved a satisfactory result either. A few days later the president categorically denied that he ever had "sexual relations" with "that woman." You remember that statement, don't you? (You probably watched that film clip about the same number of times that you saw the space shuttle explode.) In a forceful and angry tone the president demanded the ear of the American people:

> But I want to say one thing to the American people. I
> want you to listen to me. I'm going to say this again. I
> did not have sexual relations with that woman, Ms.
> Lewinsky. I never told anybody to lie, not a single time,
> never. These allegations are false, and I need to go back
> to work for the American people. Thank you.[82]

End of story, right? President Clinton denied it without
leaving any wiggle room, didn't he? Or did he? There were
no "weasel" words. Or were there? According to most of the
pundits and reporters covering the story there was enough
wiggle room to drive a truck through. It did not take long
before they began parsing this statement, alerting a wary
(or was it weary?) public that in Bill Clinton's mind oral
sex did not equal adultery. Several of his former Arkansas
state troopers have stated on the record that Clinton told
them oral sex is not the same as adultery.

Who will ever forget Ted Koppel—Dr. Dignity—intro-
ducing his *Nightline* program on January 22, 1998, by
parsing the question of oral sex and adultery?

> It may, as you will hear later in this program, ultimately
> come down to the question of whether oral sex does or
> does not constitute adultery. If the question seems both
> inappropriate and frivolous, it is neither. It may bear
> directly on the precise language of the president's
> denials. What sounds, in other words, like a categorical
> denial may prove to be something altogether different.[83]

But more troubling than Mr. Clinton's propensity for

"trimming the truth"[84] was the response of many of our fellow Americans. Time and time again we have heard people say, "I don't care if he lied about this. Can he run the economy? Can he keep Saddam in check? Can he do the job he was elected to do? He can lie all he wants to, and lie with any woman he wants to, as long as he doesn't lie down on the job. He can be 'economical with the truth'[85] as long as he is true to the economy."

In an interview on CNN, *Politically Incorrect's* Bill Maher summed up this postmodern "so what?" approach. Maher made it quite obvious that he believed that the president had engaged in a sexual relationship with Monica Lewinsky. He was asked if he presumed the president's innocence during his nightly monologue. Maher chuckled at the thought:

> Oh, no, because I definitely think he had an affair. I think there is, you know, an O.J. level of evidence there for that.[86]

But don't interpret that to mean moral outrage. Maher wasn't disturbed that the president had an affair with a 21-year-old White House intern. He was only upset that someone would dare to ask the president, "Did you have oral sex?" He complained,

> Well, why should you ask the president that? Tell me how that serves the nation in any way or what that has to do with anything.[87]

What business is that of ours, he was suggesting? Why should we care what the president does behind closed doors? But each night Maher made a contradictory business decision. Sex sells. So he poked fun at the president's sexcapades. He held the president's dirty laundry (and the office of the presidency) up for public ridicule. Doesn't that seem a little two-faced to you? If Bill Maher is allowed to joke about the president's sex life, aren't we allowed to take it seriously?

Speaking of jokes, a sick joke has been making the rounds for years. It asks the question, "How can you tell when President Clinton is lying?" Answer: "Whenever his lips are moving." In the same vein a political cartoon depicted "George Washington Clinton." Mr. Clinton was featured in one of those "Founding Father"-type powdered wigs, protesting, "I cannot tell a lie... convincingly...." [88] Does it do your heart good to see the president of the United States ridiculed as the laughingstock of the country?

Ask yourself, if Mr. Clinton looked into the camera and lied to the country about this, what else might he have lied about? Has he and his administration failed to tell us the truth about the FBI files, political payoffs to Webster Hubbell, the selling of the Lincoln bedroom, trading funds illegally with a labor union, or the flow of Chinese money into the coffers of the Democratic

National Convention? If sex, lies, and audio tapes are no big deal to the country, aren't these other gross abuses of power enough? Are we willing to allow Mr. Clinton to lie to us... convincingly? Are we willing, as Michael Kelly suggested, to be accomplices in these lies?

> But year by year, scandal by scandal, the defense of Clinton has made the rest of us accomplices to these lies....
>
> In 1992 Clinton said that his enemies were targeting him for a woman he didn't sleep with and a draft he didn't dodge. Liberals knew in their hearts that both claims were lies, but they told themselves that this didn't matter.[89]

Perhaps we should turn a blind eye to the truth and tell ourselves, "It doesn't matter." Are we willing to sit on our thumbs while lying is elevated to an art form? President Clinton and his clever handlers "have made lying such an art form," Maureen Dowd groused, "that the truth is not merely obscured. It is unattainable."[90]

Shame on him, Ms. Dowd implied. But shame on us, if we fall for it! Do we want our children to think they can lie to anyone they want to—and with anyone they want to—and still grow up to be president? Do the postmodern Clintonites win? If so, our children are the biggest losers.

Although written more than a century ago, the words of Dostoyevsky, the Russian novelist, might be the best advice President Clinton will ever receive. From *The*

Brothers Karamazov comes this mini-sermon on the importance of telling the truth. "We the people" would do well to listen and heed this:

> The important thing is to stop lying to yourself. A man who lies to himself, and believes his own lies, becomes unable to recognize the truth, either in himself or in anyone else, and he ends up losing respect for himself as well as for others. When he has no respect for anyone, he can no longer love and, in order to divert himself, having no love in him, he yields to his impulses, indulges in the lowest forms of pleasure, and behaves in the end like an animal, in satisfying his vices. And it all comes from lying—lying to others and to yourself.[91]

Do you believe this?

"Around Washington, those in awe of the President's resilience, say that if Bill Clinton were the Titanic, the iceberg would have gone down."[92]

—MARGARET CARLSON IN
TIME MAGAZINE

An "Achilles Without a Heel"?

It was America's least favorite heel who tried to convince us that Bill Clinton was invincible. Maybe that was because Dick Morris thought that he was invincible. Do you remember Mr. Morris? Of course you do. He was the toe-sucking, X-rated presidential advisor who had his own affair to remember. It was Morris who assured us that Clinton was "an Achilles without a heel." But, alas, Cupid's arrow may have found its mark, but not in Bill Clinton's heel.

This was duly noted by nationally syndicated columnist Ellen Goodman, who is no bleeding-heart conservative.

She landed a clever retort on Morris. "The heel was never the problem," she protested. It was a "zipper problem" that forced Ms. Goodman to air publicly her belief that she had been betrayed personally. "If... if... if," she cautioned. "But *if* the President had an affair with a 21-year-old intern in the White House, it isn't just his wife who's been betrayed."

Ms. Goodman was right. It wasn't just his wife who felt violated—if Hillary did experience those emotions, whch some would question. A number of other people who worked with or trusted Bill Clinton felt violated by his alleged behavior. Some went public with their frustration. Most notable among them was Clinton's former senior adviser, George Stephanopoulos. He could barely conceal his outrage as he downloaded his frustration in a *Newsweek* article entitled, "A Question of Betrayal":

> If true, the allegations about the president's relationship with Monica Lewinsky show that he failed to meet the standards of character he set for himself, and shattered the promise he made to the public and the people around him. Right now, I don't know whether to be angry, sad or both. But if the Lewinsky charges are valid, I know this: I'm livid. It's a terrible waste of years of work by thousands of people with the support of millions more.[93]

Why did Stephanopoulos react with such uncharacteristic outrage over the allegations? Because he felt that all of his efforts on behalf of the president were violated by Clinton's cavalier sexcapades with a young White House intern. "It's mystifying to me," reflected George Stephanopoulos, "that someone with so much to offer and so much to lose would risk everything in such a reckless way."[94]

Good point, George! It was senseless for a man who knew he was staring down a lawsuit for sexual harassment to get caught in a tryst with a young woman who was only a few years older than his daughter. It was unseemly to Mr. Stephanopoulos. Unfortunately, the American people did not share his outrage. "Oh, well," many of them sniffed, "boys will be boys." "Who cares how low he sinks morally," they shrugged, "as long as the Dow Jones can keep going up and up." This was the greater outrage.

On the *Today Show* Katie Couric's faith in the president was rocked by the early allegations of this sex scandal. Viewers didn't know it at the time, but Katie was wading through some deep waters of her own. Her husband, Jay Monahan, was near death. In retrospect, this only amplified her puzzled reaction concerning Clinton's recklessness. She wondered aloud on camera:

> "If the allegations are true... how is it this intelligent, ambitious, politically savvy man can be so foolhardy and such a slave to his libido?"[95]

Like George Stephanopoulos, Katie felt betrayed by the impudence of what the president was alleged to have done.

But a person's IQ has nothing to do with self-control. Our postmodern culture can't comprehend that, but it is true. Self-control is a function of conscience and a belief in absolute standards of right and wrong. If a man is "ethically challenged," no amount of brainpower can keep him from being shackled by his libido. It is the fact that "we the people of the United States of America" have forgotten this, which is so tragic.

Another one of Clinton's former aides, David Gergen, is a revolving presidential advisor. He has made a career of serving presidents in four very different administrations. He, too, found himself struggling with feelings of betrayal when he heard about Clinton's alleged sexcapades. Gergen begs the question, "Has he kept faith with us?" By that question he implied that the American people had been betrayed by the president's shenanigans. "The larger question," he scribbled, "is whether he has kept faith with the American people."

In what way did he fail to keep faith with the people?, some might wonder. Gergen spelled it out in painstaking detail:

> In electing Clinton, voters entered an implicit bargain: "We promise to forgive your past; you promise to behave in the future. If you have a psychological problem with sex, please get help." Exploiting an intern would not only be wrong but would violate the covenant.[96]

Journalist Gloria Borger, confessed that she and other reporters had made that same Faustian bargain with Bill Clinton. In the midst of all the media navel-gazing about the initial rush-to-judgment by journalists in the Lewinsky affair, Borger admitted:

> Hard as it may be to believe, journalists are the idealists in the saga of Monica and Bill. The public doesn't feel betrayed; reporters do. We're hurt, because we believed that the president promised he would not stray again. We're mad, because we've heard rumors this has not been the case and we've chosen not to pursue them.[97]

Are Ellen Goodman, George Stephanopoulos, Katie Couric, and David Gergen right when they assert that the American people were betrayed by Bill Clinton? Whether "we the people" believe it or not? Was the president's promiscuous behavior so outrageous that he failed us as our "moral leader"? One freelance writer, who sounded off in *USA Today*, disagreed. Certainly, the president would score low on a moral aptitude test, he argued. So what? "We the people," he insisted, don't elect our presidents to be our "moral leaders":

> "We'd probably give the president low marks in the morals department, but then we don't see him as our moral leader. He was elected to run the country. We'll worry about our morals ourselves, thank you very much."[98]

But is that true? Are "we the people" content to have a president with a low moral aptitude? "As long as he can run the economy, he can run around all he wants." Is that what we think? Should we be content to elect a moral nincompoop as long as he employs sound fiscal policies? What about "the children"? Most policies in the federal government today have been built upon concern for "the children." Shouldn't we be a little concerned if the president of the United States is not a good moral example for "the children"? More to the point, are we?

According to a Zogby poll taken three weeks after the Lewinsky story first broke, "we the people" do not think that Bill Clinton is a good role model for "the children." Democratic pollster Zogby concluded that "nearly two in three US voters prefer that President Clinton not be regarded as a role model for their children." On the other side of the ledger, Zogby noted, "Only one in four regard the President as a good 'personal role model' for their children."

Now that was either bad news *for* the president or bad news *about* us. It was bad news for Mr. Clinton if two-thirds of the voters were outraged to think that he was not a good example for "the children." It was bad news about us if two-thirds of the voters think the president is a lousy moral example for children, but don't give a rip as long as he can rustle up good economic indicators. Which was it?

Should we sit still "like the monkeys who see no evil, hear no evil and speak no evil?"[99] If the president of the United States is guilty of using women and then trashing them, if he is guilty of looking the American people straight in the eye and lying to them, should he be allowed to get away with this? What kind of example does this set for the next generation of leaders? If Bill Clinton has taken his inspiration from John Kennedy and this travesty is the result, what will it be like when future leaders of postmodern America take their inspiration from President Clinton? Thomas Sowell was right. "If Clinton goes unpunished, others will do the same or worse." Think about the example this leaves for others, Sowell says. Here is the real Clinton legacy:

> What is far more scary than anything Clinton has done, or has been accused of doing, is the ease with which rhetoric can distract our attention from it. Three years from now, Clinton will be gone, but what will be left behind is the knowledge of how easy it is to get away with flouting the laws of the country and the simplest rules of common decency, if one knows which rhetorical buttons to push and what words to spin.[100]

Was Dick Morris right? If Bill Clinton is an "Achilles without a heel," what kind of heels do we have to look forward to in our future presidents? Is it possible that this first postmodern president is far worse than the proverbial bull in a china shop? Is he, to borrow a line from Winston

73

Churchill, "a bull who carries his china closet with him"?[101] Meaning? Meaning that he may be on a self-destructive course. Meaning that George Stephanopolous may be quite right: he has betrayed us. Meaning that Bill Clinton may be too reckless and too cavalier to be the leader of the free world, and the leader of this "free country."

Do you believe this?
Does any of this [scandal] make a lick of sense?
Could it be that America just
loves a party animal?
—"BILL CLINTON PARTIES ON,"
NASHVILLE SCENE

"Don't Ask, Don't Tell" Doesn't Cut It!

One of the first initiatives sponsored by the Clinton White House during its first term was the "Don't ask, don't tell" policy. It demanded a change in the way that gays are treated in the military. As long as gays and lesbians don't broadcast their sexual preferences, no branch of the military has a right to ask them whether they are homosexual. It is interesting to watch Mr. Clinton adopt this same policy in dealing with scandalous allegations about his own behavior. His response has been to tell very little and duck any questions that anyone might ask him about his relationship with Monica Lewinsky, Kathleen Willey or other women who have been exploited by the president. Most people see it for what it really is: "Don't ask me about the truth, and I won't have to tell you any lies." But there are many questions he has an obligation to answer. And even more that need to be asked.

Does the president exploit women?

Can you picture the president of the United States cruising the White House intern secretarial pool? According to Nancy Gibbs of TIME magazine, the president made a habit of flirting with cute interns. "The interns didn't just work at the White House, they seemed to live there," Ms. Gibbs maintained. "And Clinton was known for hanging out at the offices and cubicles where the prettiest ones worked." One female White House staffer commented, "It's a construction-worker mentality." [102] In other words, the president is a girl watcher and a skirt chaser. Like a guy with a hard hat on the job site. Is that acceptable to "we the people"?

Dr. Harvey Greenberg, a New York psychoanalyst, claims that "narcissistic entitlement" is a common trait among powerful men. Not just guys who wear hard hats. In other words, a powerful man thinks he is entitled to dive head first into the secretarial pool. Ben Stein—an actor, writer, and armchair shrink—agrees. "This is how men in positions of power have very frequently acted toward women."[103] Excuse me, Mr. Stein. Didn't you mean to say that this is how powerful men have often exploited women? Isn't that closer to the truth?

While wondering what Hillary knows or suspects about her husband's "narcissistic entitlement," Journalist Gloria Borger asked a couple of questions that were quite revealing. One was this: "Does she know that some handlers at the White House try to keep attractive young women away from the president?" There is no doubt that White House employees, wasting the taxpayer's money, must protect unsuspecting young women from the First Lecher. What was in doubt, in Gloria Borger's mind, was whether Hillary understood that this was necessary. Perhaps she instituted the policy. A second question is equally revealing: "Does she know that he often makes passing remarks about women to staffers?"[104] It is a fact that Bill Clinton often evaluates women by their physical appearance. Do we really want a president that is on the prowl?

Worse still, are the American people ready to accept a sexual predator in the White House? As Andrew Ferguson noted in *TIME* Magazine:

If the tapes are correct... the President of the United

States is a sexual predator. The story line is boy-meets-girl, with a twist. The boy is 50 years old, married, and the most powerful and famous man in the world; the girl is by many definitions still a girl, a few years older than his daughter: 21, fresh from college, away from home, working for him without pay at her first real job. He is her boss; she is star struck. He travels in motorcades; she works as a clerk. She is flirtatious and pretty and willing, and he takes her.[105]

Of course, the standard defense of the president is that these are just allegations. Nothing has been proved about Paula Jones, Kathleen Willey, or Monica Lewinsky. But if it looks like a duck, and it walks like a duck, and it quacks like a duck, what do you suppose it could be? As Maureen Dowd hinted in *The New York Times*—hardly a right-wing tabloid—it appears that Mr. Clinton doth protest his innocence too much:

In 1992 Mr. Clinton professed his innocence about Gennifer Flowers and a gaggle of erupting "bimbos." But to be on the safe side, his campaign hired a private investigator to intimidate any women who might be thinking of coming forward with stories about dalliances, by threatening to reveal dirt about their pasts.[106]

Ladies and gentlemen, this isn't the job description of a fun-loving guy. This is the profile of a party animal who devours his prey once he is done playing with her. This is not harmless fun. This is a pattern of behavior that exploits women. What will happen if he gets away with this? "The danger here is, spare the rod, spoil the President," Maureen Dowd warned. "If he escapes again, he will grope again." But even worse, how many other men will "grope again,"[107] following the president's example of exploiting women?

Does the president exploit more than women?

Stop to think for a moment about what the allegations are in regard to Monica Lewinsky. It is alleged that the president used this young White House intern for oral sex. Monica's "presidential kneepads" indicate that she was giving pleasure, not receiving it. It was a very one-sided affair. If that isn't exploitation, what is? In a hard-hitting article entitled, "It's the Sex, Stupid," Andrew Ferguson noted:

> Much has already been made about the manner of sex described on the tapes. Not to put too fine a point on it, it is strictly one-way, designed for the maximum pleasure of the recipient. The pleasure of the giver is incidental.[108]

Does this suggest a pattern of exploitation that goes far beyond the president's behavior with women? In a surprising move, Michael Kinsley answered in the affirmative. Yes, said this representative of America's rarest of species, a proud liberal:

> [M]ost varieties of philandering by middle-aged big shots imply a willingness to use women in a way that suggests an exploitative attitude toward people in general.[109]

Isn't that interesting? Kinsley charged that President Clinton uses women and exploits people. Yet this president has demonstrated an amazing capacity to show empathy to people who are hurting. Recall his performance at the memorial service for the victims of the bombing of the federal building in Oklahoma City. He knew just what to say and do to comfort the families of the victims. How do you explain this incongruity? Is it possible for this man to be guilty of exploiting people when he is so good at acting empathetic? Yes, exclaimed Gloria Borger. It is possible for a wolf to masquerade inside a sheep's skin:

> There's a paradox about Bill Clinton. Here's a fellow with a deep and genuine empathy for people and feelings. Yet he also has a bad habit of using people and discarding them when things get tough. Short-term empathy; long-term emptiness.[110]

Is oral sex not to be confused with adultery?

Monica Lewinsky was reported to have joked on one of those infamous audio tapes that she had her own unofficial title, "Special Assistant to the President for B___ J__."[111] She also confirmed a view that Clinton's former state troopers had exposed several years ago: President Clinton does not consider oral sex to be adultery. He claims that he found that to be the case from reading the Bible. Now the standing joke is that he must have read that in St. Paul's letter to *Penthouse*.

What is truly funny about all of this is that Bill Clinton's Scripture-twisting caused the editors of *TIME* magazine to do their own Bible study on oral sex. Walter Kim reported the results, concluding that "the news is not good for the President. It's terrible." Citing Genesis 38:8-10 as relevant to the discussion, he concluded with this quote from Holy Writ: "And the thing which he did displeased the Lord: wherefore he slew him also."

Next, Kim quoted no less an authority than Jesus from the Sermon on the Mount: "But I say unto you that whosoever looks on a woman to lust after her committed adultery with her already in his heart." From that rigorous assertion Kim concluded, "This teaching appears to leave oral sex recipients no moral wiggle room..."[112] His Bible study led him to a totally different conclusion than Bill Clinton's casual Bible reading. Kim found that "the oral-sex-isn't-really-sex" distinction is found "nowhere in sacred Scripture."[113]

Apparently Mr. Kim never stumbled across St. Paul's Epistle to *Penthouse* in the course of his Bible study.

One California shrink observed that it is "common

among professional American males to view oral sex as a kind of moral freebie."[114] Many teenagers have borrowed that same rationale. Senator Charles Robb of Virginia got away with that kind of logic. After admitting to receiving a "nude massage" from another woman, Robb had the temerity to protest, "I haven't done anything that I regard as unfaithful to my wife, and she is the only woman I've loved, or slept with, or had coital relations with in the 20 years we've been married."[115] That isn't too difficult to parse, is it?

Unfortunately for Mr. Clinton and Mr. Robb, this kind of word play does not cut it in a court of law. As one New York divorce lawyer summed up the situation, "Case law has developed that says oral sex is adultery, too."[116] If men really want to know whether oral sex constitutes adultery, all they need to do is ask their wives.

Will President Clinton succeed in deceiving us?

Bill Clinton deserves a black belt in "cunning linguistics."[117] No one can deny *nothing* while attempting to deny *something* better than the acting president of the United States. Do you remember his pious and pithy denial of the alleged relationship with Monica Lewinsky? "I did not have sexual relations with that woman, Miss Lewinsky." To some who heard it, that was a forceful denial that the charges were true. To others, it was a bold-faced lie. But then it became clear to all but the very faithful Clintonites that it was something altogether different. It was pure and unadulterated deception.

As Michael Kelly discovered, there was plenty of wiggle room in that non-denial denial.

> "Sexual relations" would seem pretty much to cover everything. Actually, according to Webster's Ninth New Collegiate Dictionary, the phrase means "coitus," which in turn is narrowly defined as "physical union of male and female genitalia...." So "sexual relations" does not include, for example, oral sex.[118]

Some pundits and lawyers might profess to admire the president's cheek; that he was willing to play those kind of word games with "we the people." Most Americans, however, apparently decided to turn the other cheek. As long as he denied it we can go back to sticking our heads in the sand of our good economy, they reasoned. But to be willing to play the president's word games, Americans have to be willing to believe a lie, as Charles Krauthammer reasoned so carefully:

> The lies and half-lies, dodges and deceits, obfuscations and diversions of a lifetime have been distilled down to one: "I did not have sexual relations with that woman."
>
> To believe that this is not a lie, you have to believe that Monica Lewinsky spent 20 hours in unguarded conversation with a confidante anguishing over an affair that she wholly imagined. As a psychiatrist, I have

treated people with delusions. People that delusional are generally found muttering to themselves in the street. They do not hold down jobs and lead otherwise normal lives. They do not get top-secret Pentagon clearance. They do not have their personalities publicly deemed "impressive" by a very close friend of the president of the United States.

To believe Clinton you have to believe that he is silent about the nature of his relationship with Lewinsky because he is "gathering the facts." Gathering the facts? You'd think he was investigating some far-flung executive branch operation in the Burmese jungle. At question here, alas, is the position of the president's own zipper. He already knows the facts. Everyone knows that he refuses to disclose them not because he is gathering them but because he is creating story lines dependent on what Lewinsky testifies.[119]

Imagine for a moment what it would be like to have another O.J. Simpson loose in the country. Another devil that everybody knows is guilty, but who gets away with his dirty deed. Except that this character happens to be the primary occupant of 1600 Pennsylvania Avenue. Picture, as Charles Krauthammer did, Bill Clinton as an "Oval Office O.J.": "He'll be a dead man walking, an object of ridicule, an Oval Office O.J., denying what everyone knows he did."[120]

That will be President Clinton's legacy, if, somehow, he gets away with being a sexual predator because he had his own "Dream Team" of spin doctors and legal eagles. He has proven to be a master at word play. But will the American people play along?

Does the president believe that he is above the law?

Whether Marianne Means meant to do it or not, she cut to the heart of the debate about Bill Clinton's behavior. Characterizing the president's sexcapades as "hanky-panky with a young intern," she asked two very provocative questions:

> If it's not OK for ordinary workers to grope females on the job and lie about it, why would it be OK if the leader of the free world were guilty of similar behavior?...
> Who threw away the rule book when it came to Bill Clinton?[121]

Great questions, aren't they? What makes them so great is the fact that they leave no room for good answers.

Why should the "education president" get away with behavior for which any high school principle would be dismissed? Why does Bill Clinton always seem to get away with lowering our morality to his level? Do we really want to be ruled by a man who breaks all the rules? To borrow insight from the left and right-brained P.J. O'Rourke:

> Critics say Bill Clinton is guilty of inappropriate behavior. This isn't so. Bill is a humanist. He thinks man is the highest arbiter of right and wrong.... It is appropriate to act as though you are above the law if you're sure the law is beneath you.[122]

Does this call into question the president's judgment?

For those who insist that the president's sex life should be the "Forbidden City" of American politics, there is a nagging question. Don't President Clinton's sexcapades with a White House intern call into question his judgment? After all, he knew that he was facing a lawsuit from Paula Jones that called into question his predatory behavior. Why, as Jonathan Alter asked, take these kinds of risks?

> If true, why would he risk it all? Why would he make a mockery of campaign slogans like "personal responsibility" and "playing by the rules"? Why would he be so stupid—both before the 1996 election and after discovery began in the Paula Jones case—when he knew that there was, indeed, a long-term campaign by dedicated right-wingers to destroy him? [123]

"All of it reflects bad judgment on his part," argued one prominent Democrat who was in close contact with the White House when the Lewinsky scandal broke. "It is bad judgment for any older man to fall into that situation." [124] Or maybe it is an indication that this older man was not exercising judgment of any kind: good or bad. "When people are caught up in compulsions, they're not conscious of consequences," says New York psychologist Doug Hogan. "They describe it like being in a trance." [125] Imagine that. A president stripped of any self-control, driven by his addiction. Wouldn't you guess that could be hazardous to the country's health?

Instead of chastening him, the Gennifer Flowers brush with political death apparently emboldened him. Far beyond the sex, this is a dangerous trait in a president—to be in the grip of the irrational and get off on it.[126]

But if the president of the United States has been guilty of bad judgment, does that mean that its citizens can't exercise good judgment? How can we tolerate this kind of reckless and shameless behavior in the White House? If our first postmodern president is willing to be this reckless in his private life, how reckless might he be willing to be in his public conduct? Do we really want to find out?

Do you believe this?

*"Kenneth Starr and his cronies should
be tarred and feathered and put on
the first box car out of D.C."*[127]

—FAX TO CNN'S TALKBACK LIVE

When All Else Fails...
Attack Ken Starr

It was a magical moment of delicious irony. Did you
catch it? When the First Lady was interviewed on the *Today
Show*, she charged that a "vast right-wing conspiracy" was
responsible for her husband's legal and moral predica-
ment. That afternoon the right wheel of Air Force One got
stuck in the mud at a regional airport in Illinois. Even
Mike McCurry found humor in that. He had little else to
chuckle about in those early days of the Fornigate scandal.
As the president's press secretary he had to endure the
daily inquisition known as the White House press briefing.
But McCurry seized on the irony when he quipped, "Well,
I think at the very least we've now proved for a fact that

there certainly is a conspiracy under the right wing."[128]

Later, a political cartoonist chuckled all the way to the bank about Hillary's conspiracy theory. He sketched an angry mother confronting her naughty little boy. On the floor next to the sheepish little guy was a broken lamp. Unfortunately for him, the only explanation for the calamity that the little boy could muster was an excuse he had heard from one of the country's leading role models. "It was a right-wing conspiracy," he complained.[129] Do you think his irate mother bought this excuse? Do you suppose he was any more successful in his bid to find a scapegoat than Mrs. Clinton was?

For the most part, Americans did not buy Hillary Clinton's accusation of a right-wing conspiracy. It became a national joke. But while everybody was laughing at her, the First Lady pulled off a major sea change. "Mrs. Clinton did something very clever," explained GOP pollster Kellyanne Fitzpatrick. "She shifted the debate from right vs. wrong to right vs. left."[130] More to the point, her accusation narrowed the debate to Starr vs. Clinton. Ken Starr, she alleged, was "a politically motivated prosecutor who is allied with the right-wing opponents of my husband."[131] It was the opening shot in what became a scorched-earth battle.

After Hillary's *Today Show* interview, and following the president's "State of the Union" address, Mr. Clinton's approval ratings shot sky high. Meanwhile, Ken Starr's approval ratings tanked. His approval ratings sank to Saddam Hussein's level. It was a clever ploy by the First Lady and her team of spin doctors to change the subject. Suddenly, it was not the president's moral deficiencies but Starr's legal tactics that became the subject of media scrutiny. It was clever, but it was not kosher. "We the people" should never have allowed the Clinton team to change the subject. It was not right for the White House to attack Ken Starr. Nor was it fair. Why? Simply put, there are six good reasons why it was not appropriate for the White House to turn its big guns on Ken Starr, the independent counsel.

1. Democrats revived the independent counsel law

Have the Clintons forgotten that it wasn't the "right-wing" Republicans who generated the independent counsel law in the wake of Watergate? It was the Democrats who created this legal monstrosity that they now denigrate as the "fourth branch of government." Nor was it a Republican Congress that revived the Independent Counsel Act. It had expired in 1993, and it was President Clinton and a Democratic Congress who voted to reconstitute it. Washington insiders warned the Clinton Administration not to do it. But they did it anyway, professing that they would have the most ethical administration in history.

But now the Democrats have elected to grouch about the independent counsel for doing the task as they outlined it to be done. They complain loudly and often about the millions of dollars he has spent, although they authorized the expense. There is something very wrong with this picture. Democrats created this Frankenstein, and they applauded as it pillaged Republican administrations. But now that it is plundering one of their own they protest that the office of the independent counsel has outlived its usefulness. This is extremely hypocritical. Maureen Dowd unmasked Mr. Clinton's own hypocrisy in allowing his minions to attack Ken Starr when she observed:

> The President who professes his innocence about Monica Lewinsky now has private detectives slithering around looking for dirt on those who might harm him. Does that include Kenneth Starr and his team? That would mean the President was investigating the investigators that his own Administration had authorized.[132]

But ask yourself, why are the Democrats in Congress attacking Ken Starr? Why have they gone on the offensive? Why haven't they elected to defend the president, rather than attack Ken Starr? Could it be that they realize that Mr. Clinton's behavior is indefensible? Is it possible that their silence concerning the president's extra-curricular activities is a tacit admission of his guilt?

In the end, the president's high approval ratings will not be able to save him from a fate worse than death— living in disgrace as a presidential version of O.J. Simpson. It is now becoming very clear that the Clinton White House may go down in history as the least ethical administration of all time. They have sunk to new lows in abusing the power and influence of the executive branch. This president and his cabinet members have generated more seamy scandals than any other administration in history. Historians will have little trouble documenting these abuses. When the lawyers have filed their last briefs, Mr. Clinton will be left alone to twist in the wind. Thanks to the only verdict that matters in the long run— the verdict of history.

2. A broken pledge

In his early interviews about the Lewinsky scandal, President Clinton assured the country that he intended to fully cooperate with Ken Starr's investigation. Then he unleashed his attack dogs—James Carville, Paul Begala, and Lanny Davis—to maul the independent counsel. It wasn't a new strategy. It is the same strategy that he has employed in all of his other sex scandals. Pledge cooperation, and then savage any and all opponents.

Even one of the president's pit bulls assured the

country that the administration would cooperate with Mr. Starr. "The investigation will go on," noted Paul Begala, one of Clinton's favorite attack dogs. "It will be cooperated with fully, and at the end [of the] day he'll be cleared." [133] Does the White House really expect the American people to believe that it is fully cooperating with the investigation while it is stabbing the investigator in the back? Apparently!

If "we the people" had not been so muddled in our thinking, we would have noticed that these attacks on Ken Starr represented a promise broken by the president. Having pledged to work with the investigation, he and his cronies proceeded to undermine it. They launched a smear campaign against Starr and his staff. In these Starr wars it was the Clinton empire that struck back. By the time it was over, Starr ranked in disdain on a par with the Sheriff of Nottingham—the notorious scoundrel from the Robin Hood legends.

These partisan attacks by the Clinton team were unfair. Remember, the White House knew that Starr could not defend himself. He had to fight with both hands tied behind his back, bound by grand jury secrecy. If he did try to respond, he simply invited another tongue-lashing by the Clinton spin doctors. It was pitiful to watch Clinton's bullies bludgeon a law enforcement officer in broad daylight. All in the name of cooperation.

Without question Evan Thomas of *Newsweek* summed it up best when he predicted in advance the White House strategy: "Defense lawyers, in particular, like to obfuscate and hide the truth. I think that Clinton's defense team... will do their very best to stall and delay and to make sure we don't find out the truth."[134]

3. *Rush to Judgment*

Do you remember the rush to judgment launched by the electronic and print media after the Sexgate scandal broke? It was like a freight train thundering downhill out of control. America's favorite "talking heads" began speculating about a possible resignation. Some, like George Stephanopolous (now with *ABC News*), thrust the "I" word into the discussion, raising the specter of impeachment.

It took Hillary Clinton to stop that freight train. She and the other White House spin doctors cautioned the media and the public not to rush to judgment. Discussion of the possibility of resignation or impeachment was premature, they argued. These were only allegations, they reminded us. Which was all true. Just as suddenly as it had begun, the rush to judgment stalled regarding the president.

But the rush to judgment did not disappear. It just changed subjects. Now it was the White House attack machine that began urging the public to rush to judgment concerning Ken Starr and his tactics. What was argued as inappropriate to do to Bill Clinton was done to Ken Starr. They substituted one rush to judgment for another, and hardly anyone called them on the carpet for it.

While the spin doctors urged the media to hit the brakes concerning President Clinton, they urged the public to put the pedal to the medal in a "rush to judgment" concerning the president's chief antagonist, Ken Starr. "Don't judge the President before the facts are in," they begged the public. Yet, out of the other side of their mouths they urged the public, "Go ahead and rush to judgment about Ken Starr's tactics as an independent counsel." What was good for the goose was not good for the gander, apparently. It was glaring hypocrisy on the part of the "spin doctors." Unfortunately, they pulled it off. To their shame and ours.

4. Mr. Starr's staff is qualified

Lost in all of the rhetoric and spin about Ken Starr is the fact that this independent counsel has a great reputation as a fair and impartial judge. "Starr—who is... fundamentally an honorable man... does not deserve the trashing he has been taking," complained Stuart Taylor as the Starr wars heated up, "especially from people desperate to divert attention from the evidence implicating Clinton in serious federal crimes." Taylor, a highly respected legal correspondent for the *National Journal,* added this testimonial concerning Starr's tactics:

> Kenneth W. Starr has done almost everything right, as best I can tell, ever since Linda Tripp dumped the Monica Lewinsky mess in his lap on Jan. 12.[135]

One of President Clinton's former White House advisors, David Gergen, gave this testimony concerning Mr. Starr's character and conduct: "Judge Starr built a sterling reputation for honesty as a judge on the federal court of appeals," Gergen noted, as if he were reading from Starr's resume, "and then as solicitor general of the United States." Then Gergen assured readers of *U.S. News & World Report* that "Sam Dash, Democratic counsel during the Ervin investigation of Richard Nixon, is Starr's ethics adviser and in private speaks well of him."[136]

Another former Clinton sidekick echoed Gergen's assessment of Starr. This time it was the president's former chief-of-staff, Leon Panetta. He begged the president to call off his attack dogs. Conceding that Mr. Starr has "made some mistakes in the way he's handled some of the issues here," Panetta gave this piece of advice to the White House and to the nation:

> [B]ut at the same time, he's somebody that does have a good reputation in Washington, and I think that he's

got to be given an opportunity to investigate the situation.... Give him the room to do it.[137]

Panetta was right. Ken Starr probably made mistakes in conducting his investigation into the Clintons. But they were technical mistakes, not violations of the law. Unfortunately, the Clinton team was only too happy to magnify Starr's blunders to provide cover for the president's legal and ethical violations. By pointing out the sawdust specks in Starr's eye, the Clinton spin doctors turned the country's attention away from the four-by-four lumber in the president's eye. "We the people" fell for this gimmick. Shame on us!

History will be much kinder to Ken Starr than it will be to Bill Clinton. Perhaps the worst thing that will be said for Mr. Starr is that he was no match for the political savvy and forked-tongue rhetoric of the Clinton attack dogs. He lost the public relations war. But the president has lost much more than that. He has lost any chance of enjoying the glorious legacy that has been so near and dear to him. If Mr. Clinton is remembered for beating Ken Starr on the public playground, he will be remembered as a two-fisted bully who bloodied a fine civil servant.

5. *Too much like Nixon*

Do you remember arguments like this used to discredit Mr. Starr's investigation as a partisan attack?

> Those embittered critics of this administration and this party who could not discredit us at the polls in November will make every effort—no matter how reckless—to discredit us now. [138]

Doesn't that sound a lot like something Paul Begala might have said on *Larry King Live* some night in February 1998? It wasn't. It was actually Spiro Agnew, Richard Nixon's vice president, grousing after Watergate began to heat up.

Can you recall "the ragin' Cajun," James Carville, spouting this kind of rhetoric in defense of President Clinton?

> People are sick and tired of hearing about it. Rightly or wrongly, the people think it's much ado about nothing, that it's a political vendetta. They feel the economy, inflation, the fuel shortage, things like that, overshadow the importance of Watergate. [139]

It wasn't James Carville, however. It was Senator Jesse Helms a quarter of a century ago complaining that Watergate didn't matter. All that mattered, Helms argued in vain, was the state of the economy. Apparently, Sir James ripped a page out of Jesse Helms' play book and added his own Cajun spin to it.

This is one more reason why President Clinton and his spinmeisters were foolish to launch a smear campaign against Ken Starr. It may save the president's bacon in the short term, but he will look like a political hog in the long term. "Slick Willy" will have the glorious distinction of ranking with "Tricky Dick" in the presidential hall of shame. It is not a comparison that would make any mother proud.

6. *Trashing the law*

This whole "Starr Wars" episode will prove to be a sorry chapter in American jurisprudence. But Ken Starr will not be the goat in the history books. It will be the Clintons and their blatant disdain for the law that will be chastised. The Clintons preach by their own example that if you get caught breaking the law, just break the back of the law enforcement officials. As David Gergen described it:

> But the relentless efforts to smear Starr as "corrupt" and as the leader of a right-wing conspiracy are unfair to the man and unseemly for a White House that is supposed to promote respect for the law.[140]

But what Gergen left unsaid is even more appalling than what he said. Not only has the president showed a blatant disrespect for the law, he has taught the American people to have a blatant disrespect for those charged to uphold the law. He made the American people and their high approval ratings his co-conspirators in attacking Ken Starr. He could argue, "The more my people attacked Starr, the more the people approved of me. It's their fault."

Future generations will not excuse President Clinton's

naughty behavior because the economy was good in the 1990s. Once we have crossed his celebrated "Bridge to the 21st century" it will not be Bill Clinton's impact on the economy that historians will discuss. In fact, it is doubtful that he will get much credit for that. Alan Greenspan will steal that show. It will be his demeaning of the office of the presidency and his abuse of the judicial system (including Mr. Starr) that will be the talk of the town.

Someday, a tell-all book will be written about Ken Starr's investigation. Maybe Starr will write it himself. Perhaps it will be part of his memoirs. But the book will be an instant bestseller. "We the people," the characters who have lived through this sorry chapter of American history, will gobble up that book. People who turned a deaf ear and a blind eye to Clinton's legal maneuvers will be stunned by the corruption that Ken Starr was charged to investigate. In the final analysis, ladies and gentlemen, it will be the disapproval ratings of historians that will get the last laugh.

In the future we will be told that acquiring more than 900 FBI files was just part of a pattern of a horrible abuse of power by the Clintons. We will discover that the harassment of the travel office employees—especially Billy Dale—after they were fired was a terrible abuse of power of the executive branch of government. We will discover that Mr. Clinton was very much aware of where the money raised by John Huang and Charlie Trie was coming from. All of this and much, much more will become "perfectly clear." By that time it will be too late to strip Mr. Clinton of the presidency. But it will not be too late to strip him of the real prize: his legacy.

If the Clinton attack machine wins, justice will lose. Not the Justice Department, which appoints an independent counsel. But justice itself. Maybe justice is blind. But the American people had better be able to see through what has taken place. We have been eyewitnesses to a postmodern power trip. As one critic of the postmodern credo—truth is an exercise of power—wrote:

> Those who rule impose their constructions of reality on everyone else.... Today, academic politics has become notoriously nasty, replacing genteel discussion with vicious personal attacks on one's opponents. Similarly, in Washington, the best way to reply to a charge is not to address whether or not it is true but to slander, indict, investigate, or otherwise crush the people who are making it.[141]

Bludgeon your opponent. Win at all costs. Truth doesn't matter. Survival does. Whatever it takes to outlast your opponent is all that matters. Winning isn't everything. It's the only thing.

Welcome to the postmodern world.

Do you believe this?

"President Clinton announced it today.
The first balanced federal budget in 30 years.
To give you an idea how long ago this is—the last
time we had a balanced budget, many of the
President's mistresses were not born."[142]

—BILL MAHER ON *POLITICALLY INCORRECT*

Is the Presidency a Joke, or Just This President?

How could anybody not be just a little curious to tune in after Larry King announced that his guest the next night would be Bill Bennett? Bill Bennett, the author of *The Book of Virtues* and brother to Bob Bennett, President Clinton's lawyer. One of the interesting sidebars in the story of the Civil War has always been the clash of brother against brother. Larry King was offering the country—and the world—a Kodak moment featuring the clash between two brothers in America's culture wars. If Charles Dickens were alive today, he might have found fodder for a blockbuster novel, *A Tale of Two Brothers.*

Here in one family is a microcosm of the whole country, divided by the "he said/she said" debate. One brother, Bill, protesting that despite the president's "lawyerly" denials, he—and nearly everyone he had talked to—did not believe them. And the other brother, Bob, the president's lawyer, protesting that the president says he hasn't done these things and assuring us that he believed him. Amazing!

For those who did tune in to *Larry King Live* the next night, Bill Bennett did not disappoint. He made several candid remarks about Washington's latest and greatest sex scandal, including an alarming observation that no matter what people think about the merits of the allegations, they tend to believe them.

> You know, I've been going around the country the last two or three days, and there's lots of opinions on this. There are lots of polls on this. Some people care a lot, some people don't seem to care a lot. I have heard a lot of things. I have not heard a lot of the following: I have not heard a lot of people say, "I just don't think he's the kind of guy to have done this sort of thing." Unfortunately, by Bill Clinton's history, a history of intrigues and dissembling about them, the current situation is plausible. When you add to that the facts, it becomes more plausible.[143]

But Bill Bennett was bothered by another troubling side to everything that he was hearing in his travels: the tawdry jokes and the high-powered debates. He looked into the camera and expressed regret that the president was not getting one particular piece of advice that he desperately needed. Certainly not from his lawyers. Not even from Bill's brother, Bob. He spelled out that advice for Mr. Clinton:

> But the one thing, perhaps, no one has said to him is the following: Mr. President, you're the president of the United States. You're not just a defendant. You're not just the accused. You're the symbol and leader of this world, of this country. Do you have any idea what's going on in this country? The conversations that are going on, the questions?...

[Larry interrupted at this point]

What an interesting remark! "Mr. President," Bennett was saying, "you are the butt of the jokes! You are dragging the reputation of the presidency through the mud along with your own. Do you understand that?" In essence, Bennett was asking, "Doesn't that bother you, Mr. President?"

Then dawn broke the next day. Hard on the heels of Bennett's interview *USA Today* ran a fitting cover story. It was about, of all things, "Risque talk... in the workplace." It almost seemed as if the editors of *USA Today* decided to document Bill Bennett's concern about the hot topic of conversation in America: Bill Clinton's sordid sex life. Here is part of what they reported:

> The workplace is rife with raunchy jokes and stinging opinions about the Clinton sex scandal, prompting unprecedented office free-for-alls about sexual practices, infidelity and morals.
>
> Employees are checking salacious Internet sites, meeting over coffee to dish up the latest updates and swapping lewd jokes via e-mail.
>
> [S]ex jokes are flying around staid offices. Employees are debating which sex acts amount to adultery and taking sides in a national he-said-she-said dispute.[144]

Bill Bennett's point exactly! President Clinton was the butt of some of the crudest jokes ever exchanged in the lunchroom. *USA Today* offered this small sample of some of the jokes that were fit to print off the Internet:

> Why did Bill Clinton cross the road?
> *To meet some chicks.*
> Why is Clinton so interested in Middle East events?
> *He thinks the Gaza Strip is a topless bar.*
> Why was it difficult for Clinton to fire the intern?
> *He couldn't give her a pink slip without asking her*
> *to try it on.*

Those were the jokes that were fit to print. But are they jokes fit for the dignity of the office of the president of the United States? A senator from Mr. Clinton's own political party told his own sick joke about the president: It seems that President Clinton and one of his colleagues in the Senate were talking about their wives. The senator blushed as he admitted to the president that he and his wife had *not* had sex before their marriage. Then the lawmaker asked Bill Clinton, "How about you?" To which the president replied, "I don't know. What was your wife's maiden name?" [145]

President Clinton has become the laughingstock of the United States. It would be a small stretch to suggest that the presidency itself has become a joke. Have you watched the *Tonight Show* at all during either of President Clinton's terms in office? Jay Leno has treated the country to a parade of jokes about the president's sex life for almost six years. It only intensified after the Fornigate scandal broke. Few of Leno's jokes about Clinton's sexcapades would have any hope of surviving the president's own V-chip rating system.

Consider this wisecrack, which wouldn't have survived Clinton's own censorship system. Just after the Lewinsky scandal broke, Leno quipped, "Al Gore is just an orgasm away from the presidency." [146] Here is another example of one of Leno's jokes at the president's expense. This one might have survived the V-chip, but Mr. Clinton's status as the moral leader of the country cannot survive jokes like this. Leno spoofed:

Mike McCurry said today the president denies ever

> having an affair with this woman and he is going about his normal daily routine. Denying having an affair with a woman pretty much *is* Clinton's normal daily routine.[147]

Please keep this in mind: these wisecracks are being made at the expense of the man who serves as president of the United States. It is the presidency that comedians are trashing with jokes like this, not just the president. It is the presidency that is being demeaned, thanks to the sexcapades of Bill Clinton. How can anyone argue any longer, at least with a straight face, that character does not matter?

Jokes are flying. You must have heard this one: "Did you hear about Hillary's latest book? *It Takes a Village to Watch My Husband.*" Or maybe you heard this one? In a survey of American women, when asked, "Would you sleep with President Clinton?" —86 percent replied, "Not again."[148]

These jokes are funny. You can't help but laugh at them. But, on second thought, they aren't funny. As a friend of mine once remarked about University of Georgia football, this is "as serious as church." It is not a laughing matter. Think about what people are willing to tolerate in this president. In disgust Mike Barnicle of the *Boston Globe* told his readers:

> I mean, if the guy came on TV as part of a naked three-person Olympic luge team—the head of state

sandwiched inbetween two babes from Baywatch—
he'd probably crack 90 percent in the polls. Clearly, the
country is equipped to handle and applaud anything....

Today, Clinton could stand on the South Lawn
surrounded by rumors involving Sharon Stone, one
French horn, two sheep, a quart of Wesson oil, a pair of
handcuffs, a dog collar, and Donna Shalala, and people
would say: "He's my main man."

How great is this? In less than a month, Clinton has
done for adultery what John Goodman did for
cholesterol: Give it a good name.[149]

Likewise, in *U.S. News & World Report* Michael Gerson
wondered aloud whether Bill Clinton is presiding over
"the deconstruction of presidential prestige":

If the president toughs it out against evidence that
becomes overwhelming, and even manages to maintain
respectable approval ratings, there will still be
immense collateral damage to the office he holds and
the society he serves. Insofar as the presidency is
elevated by its dignity, President Clinton will leave it
diminished—miniaturized by unprintable jokes.[150]

Humor is a tool often employed by Hollywood script-
writers and producers to water down our convictions.
They know that what we laugh at, we may be willing to
tolerate. One scriptwriter admitted that his goal is to get
people to laugh at adultery, homosexuality, and incest.
From his perspective, "If you can get them to laugh at
these things, it breaks down their resistance to them."[151]

While we are laughing at TV sitcoms, somebody is playing a deadly game with our minds.

Maybe we need to heed the warning from the incomparable C.S. Lewis. He noted that "We laugh at honor and are shocked to find traitors in our midst."[152] Isn't that precisely what is happening now? As we chuckle about this postmodern president's peccadilloes, we forget that he has betrayed his oath of office. Sadly, the Clinton presidency has degenerated into a very bad joke. Unfortunately, the joke is on us.

Do you believe this?

*"The former intern was cleared to dash
over to the White House 37 times, probably
more often than the budget director but less
often than Johnny Chung."*[153]

—MAUREEN DOWD

Sexgate or Watergate II?

Can you believe it? Monica Lewinsky, the former White House intern who was the heart and soul of Sexgate, lived in the Watergate complex. Watergate, a name that will forever be linked to the death of a presidency. Maybe now two of them. Then there is Ashley Raines, the other White House intern, who reportedly corroborated Monica's story about her sexscapades with the president. Ashley's mother, it turns out, is the manager of the Excelsior Hotel in Little Rock. Never heard of it? Sure you have! It was in a hotel room at the Excelsior that Bill Clinton made his unwelcome sexual advances to poor Paula Jones. Some intriguing connections, don't you think?

But if you connect the dots, what do you get? A titillating sex scandal, and nothing more? Is it merely of passing interest that Ms. Lewinsky lived at the Watergate? Or was that an omen? The original Watergate was about a break-in. Could it be that its sequel, Watergate II, is about a live-in? Is the Lewinsky scandal just about sex, as all of the president's men have charged? Or is it about a disturbing pattern of an abuse of power that rivals Watergate, and perhaps transcends it? Could it be that the Jones/Lewinsky/Willey scandal is the tip of an iceberg that will sink Bill Clinton's legacy, if not his presidency?

Perhaps the editors of *U.S. News & World Report* subconsciously tipped the public off to the answer to that question. They helped to connect the dots between the Lewinsky scandal and other Clinton scandals. They did it with a seemingly harmless wisecrack:

> Some 1996 campaign donors paid $50,000 or more for their single up-close-and-personal visits to the White House. Monica Lewinsky got about 30, and she paid only a modest $250.[154]

Maybe that quip would have been more funny, if this whole affair (pardon the double entendre) wasn't so deadly serious. As this light jab below the president's belt intimated, there is a connection between the campaign finance abuses of the Clinton White House and the campaign of obfuscation and distortion that followed the revelations of Monica Lewinsky and Kathleen Willey. It has been the practice of this White House to stonewall investigators, deceive the public, and attack anyone who raises legitimate questions about the president's scandalous behavior. Watergate was not about the break-in. It was about the cover-up. Whitewater and Watergate II are not about the live-in. Sadly, they are all a massive and impressive campaign to cover up the truth.

But what if the Lewinsky scandal was just about sex? Is it no big deal for the president of the United States to use the sexual favors of a 21-year-old White House intern to satisfy his desires? Is that irrelevant, because a president's sexual activities are off limits? Who are we kidding—aside from ourselves, that is? What if he had engaged in sexual activity with a 12-year-old girl? Would we still say that is none of our business? Hardly!

Some people might be thinking, "I can accept the president using a 21-year-old intern to service his sexual desires. After all, what he does behind closed doors is his business." But I could not accept him using a 12 year-old girl to do the same thing," these same people might object. "It is one thing to accept that the president is a sexual predator," these people would say. "But it is quite another thing to allow a pedophile to occupy the Oval Office."

But can't these people see that they have revealed much more about who and what they are than they revealed about President Clinton? They have informed us that they put a low price on morality. All that is left to determine is how low they are willing to go?

Have you ever heard the twisted tale about the man who was chit-chatting with an attractive young woman in a fancy restaurant? In the course of the conversation, he pointed to a well-dressed young man seated at a corner table.

> "Do you see that fellow over there?" he asked. "If he offered you five thousand dollars to spend the night with him tonight, would you do it?" "For five thousand dollars?" the woman responded in astonishment. "Well, for five thousand dollars, I guess I would."
>
> A few moments later the man pointed to a distinguished gentleman seated in the opposite corner of the restaurant. "How about that guy? Suppose he offered you one hundred dollars to spend the night with him. Would you do it?" "One hundred dollars?" the girl sniffed. "Of course not. What do you think I am, a whore or something?"
>
> "Oh, we've already established that fact," the man chuckled. "I was just trying to establish your price!"

How low are some people willing to stoop in defense of this president? What about members of the president's own party? As Bill Maher put it, there is an O.J. level of evidence to suggest that the president did have a White

House intern put on her "presidential kneepads." Whether or not it will ever be proven in a court of law is yet to be seen. The fact is, it has already been proven in the court of public opinion. No one really believes that Monica Lewinsky returned to the White House 37 times to visit Betty Currie. So where is a Democratic version of Howard Baker when we need one?

Rather than reproach the president, or even defend him, those Democrats who have spoken out have gone on the offensive. They cannot defend the president's behavior. So they have elected to attack Ken Starr instead. Shouldn't there be a few Democrats who are willing to abandon the short-term good of the party for the long-term good of the country? Instead, they have closed ranks to protect President Clinton during this scandal and all of the other ones. It might be a strategy that will save the president, a fellow Democrat. But will it doom the country? How low are Democrats willing to go for their president, despite the great harm his behavior has done to the presidency?

Some pundits have observed that these sex scandals are a Rorschach test for the country. Are they also a Rorschach test for the Democratic Party? Consider the response of Nancy Pelosi, a congresswoman and a Democrat from California. She was asked by Tim Russert on *Meet the Press* whether the allegations that the most powerful boss in the free world had exploited a 21-year-old female intern for sexual favors raised questions about Mr. Clinton's treatment of women. "No, no," objected Pelosi. "They raised questions about Ken Starr's treatment of women." Did you get that?

"There's a point of sensitivity that women have about Kenneth Starr's attitude toward women," Pelosi added, trying to keep a straight face, "how he's investigating, exploiting Monica Lewinsky, how he used Linda Tripp to do that." That might seem like a pretty big stretch, but Pelosi pulled further. "The Susan McDougal case comes back to mind," she noted, "because here again is a humiliation of a woman because she won't tell him what he wants to hear in that case." Shame on Ken Starr, she pleaded. Then shamelessly she added, "And now you see the humiliation of Betty Currie."

Michael Kelly didn't stoop to dignify her remarks with his response. Kelly, who is hardly a card-carrying member of the right wing, responded to Pelosi with indignation:

> Yes, Susan McDougal was humiliated, and so was Betty
> Currie. But the agent of their humiliation wasn't Ken
> Starr; it was Bill Clinton. And he is the agent, too, of the
> humiliation of Nancy Pelosi.[155]

Perhaps, too, Mr. Clinton has been the agent of the humiliation of Pelosi's fellow Democrats. Shame on Ms. Pelosi for savaging the law in defending a man who is trying to skirt it! Shame on her fellow Democrats for conspiring to do the same thing! Will there be anyone who will rise up from the ranks of the Democrats who will cry, "Enough is enough!"? Is there anyone among them willing to sacrifice the short-term good of the party for the long-term benefit of the country?

As most people know, Sexgate goes far beyond sex. "Tripp's story, and Lewinsky's statements on tapes," legal analyst Stuart Taylor noted, "resonated powerfully with the many allegations of efforts to cover up other matters Starr was investigating." How potent was this connection to other allegations? Taylor tested his thesis by asking Clinton-appointed prosecutors this simple question: "What should Starr have done?" In other words, presented with the tapes from Tripp, what was Starr obligated to do? These prosecutors, with a bias for the president, handed Stuart Taylor a unanimous verdict:

> I posed this question to a number of high-level Clinton appointees and former Clinton appointees with extensive prosecutorial experience. They all said that— even though perjury is rarely prosecuted in civil cases—Tripp's allegations warranted aggressive criminal investigation, and that the wiring of Tripp to seek more taped evidence from Lewinsky was justified.[156]

Why was it justified? Because Sexgate and Hubbellgate and Travelgate and Filegate and Chinagate and Teamstergate all illustrate a consistent pattern of abuse of power.

Whether that is ever proven to the satisfaction of the electorate is irrelevant. Historians will wrap it all up into one huge bundle that will likely overshadow Watergate.

One journalist, in anticipation of that bundle of scandals, has already supplied the string. If you have wondered what the history books will have to say about Sexgate, think again. Historians will record, as Michael Kelly has already written, that the Lewinsky affair was not about sex. It was far more serious than that:

> The Lewinsky matter is not about the minor and personal question of whatever an individual does in the pursuit of happiness behind closed doors. And it is not about the diversionary question of prosecutorial misconduct. It is about the largest, most central and most public of questions: whether we demand that the president obey the law, whether we accept that the president lies to us....
>
> You have to tell the truth under oath, and so does the president. You may not conspire to obstruct justice, and neither may the president. You must not paw women who come to you seeking employment, and so too must not the president. To excuse the head of government from the laws that govern the rest of us is not to tolerate one man's peccadilloes; it is to tolerate the corruption of democracy.[157]

In his first inaugural address President Clinton promised us the most ethical administration in history. He may have delivered the polar opposite. His may prove to be the most ethically challenged administration of all time.

Including Warren Harding's, and yes, even Richard Nixon's. Scoff if you want to. When all of the emotional smoke and mirrors attached to all of these allegations have dissipated, the Clinton White House will be nothing but ashes. Wouldn't it be wonderful if the passing of the first postmodern president would signal the death of postmodernism as well?

Years ago I was sitting in a restaurant, minding my own business, enjoying a lunch break. I wasn't eavesdropping but I couldn't help but overhear the conversation of two young women who were sitting behind me. The one young lady told her friend about an occasion several years before when a man had invited her to spend the night at his beach house. She said that she admitted to him, "I can't, I'm too scared." But then she confided to her female companion, "But now, I probably would have accepted his offer. I'm a little older now and a little more vile."

As a nation we are a "little older" than we were in the good old days of Watergate. But aren't we also a good deal "more vile," too? Welcome to the birth of postmodernism! Wouldn't it be nice if this infantile pattern of thinking would experience a crib death?

Conclusion

Alexis de Tocqueville was one of the most enthusiastic tourists to ever grace our shores. This perceptive Frenchman toured the United States in 1835, chronicling his stimulating discoveries. One of his most famous dictums appeared at first glance to be a wonderful compliment. In reality it embodied a colossal warning:

> I sought for the greatness and genius of America in her commodious harbors and ample rivers, and it was not there. Not until I went into the churches of America and heard her pulpits aflame with righteousness did I understand the secret of her genius and power.... America is great because she is good, and if America ever ceases to be good, she will cease to be great.

By changing just two words in Monsieur de Tocqueville's thesis, it is crystal clear that President Clinton's Sexgate scandal has demonstrated that Americans may no longer be able to tell good from evil. We appear to have a moral deficit disorder. Substitute the word *moral* for the word good and this is what we would read: "America is great because she is *moral,* and if America ceases to be *moral,* she will cease to be great."

Have "we the people" ceased to be able to tell good from evil? If a 50-something president employing a 21-year-old intern for sexual favors doesn't constitute an immoral act for most Americans, then what does? Isn't that frightening evidence that the citizens of this country are suffering from a moral deficit disorder? If we can no longer recognize evil, can it be long before we cease to do good?

According to syndicated columnist Georgie Anne Geyer this disgusting Oval Office behavior is a mirror for "we the people." If most Americans are prepared to shrug off these "White House shenanigans," she queried, will we be satisfied with our reflection? Geyer scribbled:

> But what one can say, even now, is that if the American people really do feel this way, if the behavior of any American president indicates severe character flaws and we prefer to deny or ignore them, then we are facing quite a different America....
>
> If indeed few of us really do care about a president's

honor, that will show us clearly the degree to which Americans have relativized their own morality....[158]

In postmodern America, moral relativists like to pontificate, "there are no absolutes." Which is comical, since that statement is an absolute in itself. But if there are no absolute standards, then how do we determine what is right and wrong?

Answer? We take opinion polls. If you want to know whether capital punishment is right or wrong, take a poll. Find out what a majority of Americans think about capital punishment. Whatever the largest number of people think, that is what is considered acceptable for society for now. But beware, that standard could change with the next opinion poll. Absolute standards of right and wrong have been jettisoned.

If a majority of Americans don't think that what the president did is wrong, then it is acceptable. As long as the economy is good. If the economy goes into the tank, beware! Then public opinion might determine that sex with a White House intern is wholly unacceptable. The very same behavior would then be grounds for impeachment. There is a word for this postmodern pollster-generated morality: Fickle. It is also hopelessly flawed. As *Washington Post* pundit Richard Cohen noted, with tongue in cheek, "If vast majorities of Americans said Thomas Jefferson was the first president, that would not make it so."[159]

Ah, there's the rub. Facts and reality get in the way. Do you remember the old saying? "Don't confuse me with the facts, my mind is made up." That is a mandate of almost biblical proportions in this postmodern era. Truth is a matter of interpretation for thoroughly postmodern Millies. This was illustrated quite clearly several years ago. In the startling book, *The Day America Told the Truth*, the two authors took the moral pulse of America in the early 1990s. Here was one of their most newsworthy and most alarming conclusions:

> Americans are making up their own rules, their own laws. In effect, we're all making up our own moral codes. Only 13 percent of us believe in all of the Ten Commandments. We choose which laws of God we believe in. There is absolutely no moral consensus in this country as there was in the 1950s, when all our institutions commanded more respect. Today, there is very little respect for the law—for any kind of law.[160]

Now do you get it? What Bill Clinton did or did not do with Monica Lewinsky, Paula Jones, or Kathleen Willey is none of our business. If President Clinton used a White House intern as a sexual surrogate, so what? As long as the approval polls are at an all-time high, he can get away with it. It becomes acceptable behavior. Regardless of the Ten Commandments. Regardless of any and all other standards of law and morality that have held this republic together for 200 years. Wrong is all right, as long as a majority says it is. Right? Wrong!

More than a decade ago Ted Koppel of *Nightline* spoke at the commencement exercises at Duke University. What he said that day shocked his audience. It may surprise you. He took issue with the ship of state drifting into a post-modern fog. His observations and recommendations are the only sensible correction to get us back on course. Please read this carefully. (Maybe you should read it twice!)

> In the place of truth we have discovered facts; for moral absolutes we have substituted moral ambiguity. We now communicate with everyone and say absolutely nothing. We have reconstructed the Tower of Babel and it is a television antenna, a thousand voices producing a daily parody of democracy in which every-
> o one's opinion is afforded equal weight regardless of substance or merit....
>
> We have actually convinced ourselves that slogans will save us. Shoot up if you must, but use a clean needle. Enjoy sex whenever and with whomever you wish, but wear a condom. No! The answer is No! Not because it isn't cool or smart or because you might end up in jail or dying in an AIDS ward, but No! because it's wrong....
>
> In its purest form, truth is not a polite tap on the shoulder. It is a howling reproach. What Moses brought down from Mount Sinai were not the Ten Suggestions. They are commandments. Are, not were. The sheer brilliance of the Ten Commandments is that they codify in a handful of words acceptable human behavior, not just for then or now, but for all time.[161]

Thank you, Mr. Koppel. It is hard to imagine a better remedy for our postmodern moral deficit disorder. Judged by those standards, what the president of the United States has done is morally reprehensible. Whether the economy is sound or sour.

He has been on the prowl like a sexual predator, taking advantage of women by taking advantage of his power and influence.

Thomas Reeves warned us of the danger. In his outstanding analysis of the reckless and ridiculous behavior of John F. Kennedy, Reeves advised Americans to learn a lesson from Kennedy's legacy:

> The presidency is venerated by Americans in all walks of life; the inhabitant of the Oval Office is supposed, at best, to reflect our highest virtues and at the very least be trustworthy....
>
> During the Thousand Days, Kennedy arrogantly and irresponsibly violated his covenant with the people. While saying and doing the appropriate things in the public light, he acted covertly in ways that seriously demeaned himself and his office. He got away with it at the time, and the cover-up that followed kept the truth hidden for decades. That this could happen again makes it imperative that we search for presidential candidates who can, by example, elevate and inspire the American people, restoring confidence in their institutions and in themselves.[162]

Reeves' study of JFK appeared on the market in 1991, a

year before most Americans were introduced to William Jefferson Clinton. If his words had been heeded, we would have been spared a national disgrace and embarrassment. Our national nightmare is not almost over. It has only just begun—unless we heed this warning. It is high time to impeach the postmodern morality that tries to divorce private behavior from public character.

But if it is necessary to jettison our postmodern morality, it may be equally necessary to jettison our first postmodern president.

Perhaps Oliver Cromwell's denunciation of the Rump parliament in England in 1654 may need to be applied to Mr. Clinton in 1998: "It is not fit that you should sit here any longer!... You shall now give place to better men." [163]

End Notes

1. Mimi Hall and Bill Nichols, "So, it really is 'the economy, stupid,'" *USA Today,* 2 February 1998, p. 1A.
2. Gertrude Himmelfarb, "Private Lives, Public Morality," The *New York Times,* 9 February 1998, Internet.
3. "For the Record," *National Review,* 23 February 1998, p. 8.
4. "Investigating the President: Media Madness?" *CNN Transcripts,* 28 January 1998, Internet.
5. Himmelfarb.
6. Thomas C. Reeves, *A Question of Character: A Life of John F. Kennedy,* 421. New York: The Free Press, 1991.
7. Bruce Dobie, "Bill Clinton Parties On," *Nashville Scene,* 5 February 1998, p. 7.
8. Mike Barnicle, "It's too much, this fog of fibs," *Boston Globe,* 5 February 1998, Internet.
9. "Reliable Sources," *CNN Transcripts,* 7 February 1998, Internet.
10. "Perspectives," *Newsweek,* 9 February 1998, p. 21.
11. Maureen Dowd, "The Slander Strategy," *The New York Times,* 28 January 1998, Internet.
12. Ellen Goodman, "Women lack good options on Clinton," *Columbus Dispatch,* 5 February 1998, p. 9A.
13. Reeves, p. 415.

14. "Talk Back Live," *CNN Transcripts*, 26 January 1998, Internet.
15. Ibid., 23 January 1998.
16. Mike Barnicle, "His arrogance is breathtaking," *Boston Globe*, 25 January 1998, p. B1.
17. Ibid.
18. "Talk Back Live," 27 January 1998, Internet.
19. Himmelfarb.
20. George F. Will, "A Problem of Asterisks," *Newsweek*, 2 February 1998, p. 72.
21. Dobie.
22. Bruce Handy, "Oh, Behave!," *TIME*, 2 February 1998, p. 55.
23. Suzanne Fields, "Changing times, changing standards," *Washington Times*, 2 February 1998, Internet.
24. Dobie.
25. Paul F. Boller, *Not So!*, New York: Oxford University Press, 1995, p. 230.
26. Fields.
27. Dobie.
28. "Talk Back Live," 26 January 1998, Internet.
29. Fields.
30. "Talk Back Live," 26 January 1998, Internet.
31. Reeves, p. 418.
32. David Broder, "This nation deserves better of its leaders," *The Columbus Dispatch*, 25 January 1998, p. 3B.
33. Reeves, p. 415.
34. Ibid., p. 419.
35. "Talk Back Live," 23 January 1998, Internet.
36. David Maraniss, "First Lady's Energy, Determination Bind Power Partnership," *The Washington Post*, 1 February 1998, p. A01.
37. Ibid.
38. Joe Klein, "An American Marriage," *The New Yorker*, 9 February 1998, p. 34.
39. "Investigating the President: Right-Wing Conspiracy?," CNN & Company, 27 January 1998, Internet.
40. Gloria Borger, "Scenes from a marriage," *U.S. News & World Report*, 2 February 1998, p. 32.
41. Klein, p. 35.
42. Noemie Emery, "All the President's Women," *The Weekly Standard*, 9 February 1998, p. 22.

43. Barbara Lippert, "The Hillary Mystique," *New York Magazine*, 9 February 1998, p. 25.
44. John McCaslin, "Inside the Beltway: Morris' musings," *The Washington Times*, 28 January 1998, Internet.
45. Lippert.
46. Margaret Talbot, "Wife Story: The Hypocrisy of Hillaryism," *The New Republic*, 16 February 1998, Internet.
47. Dowd, "The Slander Strategy."
48. Talbot.
49. Ibid.
50. Barbara Ehrenreich, "The Week Feminists Got Laryngitis," *TIME*, 9 February 1998, p. 68.
51. Talbot.
52. Lippert, p. 25.
53. Talbot.
54. Nancy Gibbs, "Truth or... Consequences," *TIME*, 2 February 1998, p. 23.
55. Matthew Cooper and Karen Breslau, "For Better and for Worse," *Newsweek*, 9 February 1998, p. 41.
56. David Maraniss, *First in His Class*, New York: Simon & Schuster, 1995, p. 426.
57. Debra Smith, Columbus, "Is Clinton only man in government to stray?" *The Columbus Dispatch*, "Letters to the Editor," 7 February 1998, p. 11A.
58. Emery.
59. Ehrenreich.
60. Matthew Rees, "Toeing the Lines," *The Weekly Standard*, 9 February 1998, p. 22.
61. Ibid.
62. Wesley Pruden, "Pruden on Politics: On their knees for a president in peril," *Washington Times*, 30 January 1998, Internet.
63. Talbot.
64. Al Hunt, "Capital Gang," *CNN Transcripts*, 7 February 1998, Internet.
65. Pruden.
66. Matthew Miller, "Is Bill Clinton fit to be president? Yes," *U.S. News & World Report*, 9 February 1998, p. 35.
67. Talbot.
68. Ibid.

69. Ibid.
70. Goodman, "Women lack."
71. Ibid.
72. Dowd, "Dear Clarence," *New York Times,* 1 February 1998, Internet.
73. Dowd, "The Slander Strategy."
74. Gwen Daye Rickardson, "Clinton's problems haunt Thomas critics," *USA Today,* 12 February 1998, Internet.
75. Ehrenreich.
76. Kate O'Beirne, "Year of the Intern," *National Review,* 23 February 1998, p. 26.
77. S.C. Francois, "Letters to the Editor," *The Columbus Dispatch,* August 1996.
78. Barnicle, "His arrogance."
79. *Politically Incorrect,* 26 January 1998, transcript from Internet.
80. David Broder, "This nation deserves better of its leaders," *The Columbus Dispatch,* 25 January 1998, p. 3B.
81. Ibid.
82. "Talk Back Live," 26 January 1998, Internet.
83. "The Credibility of Monica Lewinsky," *Nightline,* 22 January 1998, transcript from Internet .
84. Barnicle, "This is not funny," *Boston Globe,* 29 January 1998, p. B1.
85. Christopher Hitchens, "Clinton's Comeuppance," *The Nation,* 16 February 1998, p. 8.
86. Maher.
87. Ibid.
88. Mike Luckovich of *Atlanta Constitution,* "Perspectives," *Newsweek,* 9 February 1998, p. 21.
89. Michael Kelly, "Making Liars of Us All," *The Washington Post,* 11 February 1998, p. A21.
90. Dowd, "Dear Clarence."
91. John McCaslin, "Inside The Beltway: Still Worth Quoting,"the *Washington Times,* 30 January 1998, Internet.
92. Margaret Carlson, "Inside the Magic Bubble," *TIME Special Report,* 16 February 1998, Internet.
93. George Stephanopoulos, "A Question of Betrayal," *Newsweek,* 2 February 1998, p. 50.
94. Stephanopoulos, p. 51.
95. Goodman, "Too many 'ifs' and oh so many allegations exist," *The*

Columbus Dispatch, 25 January 1998, p. 3B.

96. David Gergen, "Has he kept faith with us?" *U.S. News & World Report,* 2 February 1998, p. 88.
97. Borger, "Clinton's Secret Weapon," *U.S. News & World Report,* 16 February 1998, p. 20.
98. Thomas BeVier, "Folks tired of the circus," *USA Today,* 13 February 1998, Internet.
99. Thomas Sowell, "In Clinton scandals, the rush is to rhetoric and not judgment," *The Columbus Dispatch,* 10 February 1998, p. 7A.
100. Ibid.
101. David Oshinsky, "Enemies Right, Left, Everywhere," *The New York Times,* 12 February 1998, Internet.
102. Gibbs.
103. Jonathan Alter, "Clinton on the Couch," *TIME,* 2 February 1998, p. 53.
104. Borger, "Scenes from a marriage."
105. Andrew Ferguson, "It's the Sex, Stupid," *TIME,* 2 February 1998, p. 60.
106. Dowd, "D.C. Confidential," *The New York Times,* 25 February 1998.
107. Dowd, "The Slander Strategy."
108. Ferguson.
109. Michael Kinsley, "More Froggy Than the French," *TIME,* 9 February 1998, p. 40.
110. Borger, "Scenes from a marriage."
111. Gibbs.
112. Walter Kirn, "When Sex is not really having sex," *TIME,* 2 February 1998, p. 30.
113. Ibid.
114. Ibid.
115. Jan M. Faust, "Defining Sex: What's in a Word?," *ABCNews.com,* 26 January 1998, Internet.
116. Ibid.
117. Kirn.
118. Kelly, "An Emerging Strategy," *The Washington Post,* 27 January 1998, p. A17.
119. Charles Krauthammer, "The Limits of Credulity," *The Washington Post,* 30 January 1998, p. A23.
120. Ibid.

121. Marianne Means, "Clinton's popularity skews views about morality in politics," *The Columbus Dispatch,* 6 February 1998, p. 11A.
122. P.J. O'Rourke, "In Defense of Our President," *The Weekly Standard,* 9 February 1998, p. 9.
123. Alter.
124. Tucker Carlson, "The Alternative Narrative," *The Weekly Standard,* 9 February 1998, p. 20.
125. Alter.
126. Ibid.
127. "Talk Back Live," 23 January 1998, Internet.
128. "Investigating the President: Media Madness?," *CNN Transcripts.*
129. Jeff Stahler, "Perspectives," *Newsweek,* 9 February 1998, Internet, p. 21.
130. Walter Shapiro, "The 'loneliest job'-except for the lawyers," *USA Today,* 13 February 1998.
131. "Who is Ken Starr?" *Nightline,* 2 February 1998, Internet.
132. Dowd, "D.C. Confidential."
133. "Discussion on the Latest Development of White House Crisis," *Larry King Live,* CNN Transcripts, 26 January 1998, Internet.
134. Ibid.
135. Stuart Taylor, Jr., "Why Kenneth Starr Should Resign," *National Journal,* 21 February 1998, p. 386.
136. Gergen, "Wise counsel in the storm," *U.S. News & World Report,* 2 March 1998, p. 100.
137. Ibid.
138. Colbert I. King, "Ghosts of Scandals Past," *The Washington Post,* 14 February 1998, p. A29.
139. Ibid.
140. Gergen, "Wise counsel."
141. Gene Edward Veith, "A postmodern scandal," *World,* 21 February 1998, p. 24.
142. Maher, *Politically Incorrect,* 2 February 1998, Transcript from Internet.
143. Bill Bennett, *Larry King Live,* 29 January 1998, Internet.
144. Stephanie Armour, "Risque talk risky in workplace," *USA Today,* 30 January-1 February 1998, p. 1A.
145. "With Friends Like These...," *The Weekly Standard,* 23 February

1998, p. 2.

146. John O'Sullivan, "It's Not the Sex," *National Review*, 23 February 1998, p. 40.
147. "For the Record," *National Review*, 23 February 1998, p. 8.
148. McCaslin, "Inside the Beltway: Latest Survey," *Washington Times*, 30 January 1998, Internet.
149. Barnicle, "Be happy! (It's a trend)," *Boston Globe*, 10 February 1998, p. B1.
150. Michael J. Gerson, "Is Bill Clinton fit to be president? No," *U.S. News & World Report*, 9 February 1998, p. 35.
151. Haddon Robinson, ed., *Biblical Sermons*, p. 34.
152. Gerson.
153. Dowd, "Let's hope president didn't make policy with Lewinsky," *Columbus Dispatch*, 5 February 1998, p. 9A.
154. "Lewinsky's Modest Contribution," *U.S. News & World Report*, 16 February 1998, p. 20.
155. Kelly.
156. Taylor, p. 387.
157. Kelly.
158. Georgie Anne Geyer, "Where's the public cry for morality?" *The Columbus Dispatch*, 12 February 1998, p. 9A.
159. Richard Cohen, "Leaks? What About The Truth?" *Washington Post*, 10 February 1998, p. A19.
160. James Patterson and Peter Kim, *The Day America Told the Truth*, New York: Prentice Hall Press, 1991, p. 6.
161. Daniel W. Van Ness, "Saving a Sinking Society," *Discipleship Journal*, No. 44, 1988, p. 31.
162. Reeves, p. 421.
163. Will.

Index